Penguin Education

Penguin Modern Economics Texts
General Editor: B. J. McCormick

Development Economics
Editor: Peter Robson

An Introduction to Development Economics
Walter Elkan

Penguin Modern Economics Texts
General Editor: B. J. McCormick
Senior Lecturer in Economics
University of Sheffield

Development Economics
Editor: P. Robson
Professor of Economics
St Salvator's College
University of St Andrews

Econometrics
Editor: G. R. Fisher
Professor of Econometrics
University of Southampton

Economic Thought
Editor: K. J. W. Alexander
Professor of Economics
University of Strathclyde

Industrial Economics
Editor: H. Townsend
Professor of Economics,
University of Lancaster

International Economics
Editor: J. Spraos
Professor of Economics
University College London

Labour Economics
Editor: K. J. W. Alexander
Professor of Economics
University of Strathclyde

Macroeconomics
Editor: R. W. Clower
Professor of Economics
Northwestern University,
Illinois

Microeconomics
Editor: B. J. McCormick
Senior Lecturer in Economics
University of Sheffield

Political Economy
Editor: K. J. W. Alexander
Professor of Economics
University of Strathclyde

Walter Elkan

An Introduction to Development Economics

Penguin Books

Penguin Books Ltd, Harmondsworth,
Middlesex, England
Penguin Books, 625 Madison Avenue,
New York, New York 10022, U.S.A.
Penguin Books Australia Ltd,
Ringwood, Victoria, Australia
Penguin Books Canada Ltd, 2801 John Street,
Markham, Ontario, Canada L3R 1B4
Penguin Books (N.Z.) Ltd, 182–190 Wairau Road,
Auckland 10, New Zealand

First published 1973
Reprinted, with revisions 1976
Reprinted 1978

Made and printed in Great Britain by
Richard Clay (The Chaucer Press) Ltd,
Bungay, Suffolk
Set in Monotype Times

Penguin Modern Economics Texts

This volume is one in a series of unit texts designed to reduce the price of knowledge for students of economics in universities and colleges of higher education. The units may be used singly or in combination with other units to form attractive and unusual teaching programmes. The volumes will cover the major teaching areas but they will differ from conventional books in their attempt to chart and explore new directions in economic thinking. The traditional divisions of theory and applied, of positive and normative, and of micro and macro will tend to be blurred as authors impose new and arresting ideas on the traditional corpus of economics. Some units will fall into conventional patterns of thought but many will transgress established beliefs.

Penguin Modern Economics Texts are published in units in order to achieve certain objectives. First, a large range of short texts at inexpensive prices gives the teacher flexibility in planning his course and recommending texts for it. Secondly, the pace at which important new work is published requires the project to be adaptable. Our plan allows a unit to be revised or a fresh unit to be added with maximum speed and minimal cost to the reader.

The international range of authorship will, it is hoped, bring out the richness and diversity in economic analysis and thinking.

B. J. McC.

Contents

Editorial Foreword

Development economics is one of the newer branches of economics which is concerned with the explanation of underdevelopment and with a discussion of measures employed or advocated to overcome it. Viewed in this light it is essentially a branch of political economy in which political, social and institutional factors cannot be neglected.

There is a case for the view that Adam Smith was the first development economist. But although current interest in the subject has rightly directed attention to neglected 'development aspects' in the writings of a number of eighteenth and nineteenth century economists, their central interests, and those of their successors writing in the early part of the twentieth century lay for the most part elsewhere. Indeed, few of the latter were centrally interested in growth and hardly any in underdevelopment. In the last twenty years there has been a great growth of interest in this area which has accompanied the process of decolonization and which reflects the growing concern of international society with the poorer, underdeveloped, three quarters of the globe. In the course of it, development economics has emerged, not without controversy, as a separate area of study.

The author of this text brings to bear on the subject a knowledge derived from his own experience in developing countries and from his wide acquaintance with the historical experience of many countries in the development process. This gives his discussion of analyses and policies a perspective which more intensive studies frequently lack. He succeeds in providing an instructively eclectic introduction to a very large and difficult subject which can both stand on its own and also be usefully read before embarking on a study of the more specialized texts on particular aspects of development problems and policies which are concurrently appearing in this series.

P. R.

Preface

Development economics lacks an agreed syllabus. This makes it difficult to know what can be reasonably omitted but it also gives the author of a short book an excuse for his idiosyncrasies. Some of the exclusions from this book are more apparent than real. For example, there may be no chapters on capital or enterprise but the subjects themselves are not ignored. On the other hand I have deliberately omitted discussion of economic planning and foreign aid, mainly because both have become specialized subjects and the simple things to be said about them are too banal. Observant readers will also notice that Latin America receives little mention; the reason is that I am very ignorant about Latin America and it therefore seemed better to concentrate on Africa and South Asia about which I know more.

The book is in two parts, although there is no sharp division. After a preliminary chapter on the structure of underdeveloped countries, the first part deals with explanations for the persistence of low incomes and with the models and strategies of development that have been canvassed. The second part takes up particular issues of policy. Development economics addresses itself to problems facing the underdeveloped countries. It applies relevant theory to the solution of problems and there can be no question of separating theory from its applications or from policy issues as is sometimes done in other branches of economics. Many of the issues in development economics are a matter of controversy between the *cognoscenti*. That does not detract from the intrinsic merit of its propositions; on the contrary, it demonstrates that the subject is very much alive. Because it is alive and bursting at the seams, a short introductory book like this can do no more than pick out what seem to me the most interesting issues, in the hope that this will encourage readers to go more deeply into the arguments and also to move sideways into the areas that I have ignored. The list of References at the back should serve as a useful guide to further reading.

For such a short book I have spent an inordinately long time writing it and in the process have incurred many debts of gratitude. Dr Cyril Ehrlich helped me to plan the book. Dr Julian Bharier, Mrs Frances Stewart and Professor Peter Robson, the editor of this series, read most or all of it and made invaluable suggestions for improvements. David Prescott came to the rescue with research assistance at a critical juncture. Professor Alasdair MacBean made sure that I was not 'way out' in any understanding of the relationship between development and trade; and Carol Ogley typed most of the book amidst the noise and clatter of a busy departmental office. I am extremely grateful to them all.

I also owe debts of a different kind. One is to Professor P. T. Bauer of the LSE for the great stimulus he has provided to development economics over the years: stimulus rates higher than incontrovertibility! Another is to Professor G. M. Meier of Stanford, for the superb mastery of the subject displayed in his *Leading Issues in Economic Development*. Finally I would like to acknowledge how much I owe to F. J. Fisher, Professor of Economic History at the LSE.

1 Characteristics of Underdeveloped Countries

Although underdeveloped countries differ greatly from one another the one thing they have in common by definition is that the majority of their peoples have a relatively low standard of living. It is this low standard of living which underlies most of the characteristics of underdeveloped countries. This chapter begins with a description of these characteristics and then proceeds to portray the way in which underdeveloped countries differ not only from countries enjoying a higher standard of living but also from one another.

Not unnaturally, most of the populations of underdeveloped countries live in rural areas rather than in towns. People with low incomes spend a high proportion of them on food and since poor countries cannot easily import food much of the productive effort is bound to be devoted to the production, processing and distribution of food. It should not, however, be inferred from this, as is often done, that most people in underdeveloped countries are therefore totally engaged in farming. Indeed, occupational specialization is a characteristic of developed economies since the degree of occupational specialization in an economy must be a function of the extent of the market. Low incomes imply small markets and therefore a low degree of specialization. In practical terms this means that whilst most country dwellers live on farms – usually small family farms of five to ten acres – a good deal of their activity is in petty trading, carrying crops to the market or housebuilding and repair, or making clothes, activities that one does not ordinarily associate with farming.

Low income countries are by definition less developed – the fashionable term used by the United Nations to describe them[1] – but this does not imply that they are *un*developed. Develop-

1. Until 'developing' became the standard term, even though many are manifestly failing to develop on almost any criterion.

ment is of course an ambiguous and elusive word, and no definition seems entirely satisfactory. This becomes manifest the moment one makes the attempt. For example, suppose one defines development as the process by which people become better off, which is the definition that seems to accord most closely with what instinctively springs to mind. Does one then have to discuss as being 'not development' a process in which consumption is held constant whilst the capital stock is being enlarged? Clearly total output is being enlarged by the additions to the capital stock, but for the moment no one is any better off. Arguably the solution to this paradox lies in the words 'for the moment': additions to the capital stock are undertaken in the hope that this will ultimately lead to a greater increase in consumer goods and services or 'wage goods', than would have been available if all increases in production had been applied directly and immediately to increases in consumption. But there is always an element of gambling in capital formation: the investment may not pay off, or it may pay off only much later than anticipated. What is, however, beyond dispute is that irrespective of the outcome of an act of capital formation, something, which for want of a better word may have to be called 'development', has taken place. If that is accepted, then the simple definition of development as a process by which people become better off will not do.

Nor is this logic-chopping: both the Soviet Union between 1928 and the war and India between 1950 and the mid 1960s have experienced stagnation of consumption side by side with the very active pursuit of capital formation. In both countries capital formation has been largely channelled into the creation of 'machines to make machines' – the setting up of heavy engineering plants, steel mills and cement works, none of which produce anything that can be directly consumed; they do not even produce consumer goods factories. The argument has, of course, been that to have such capital goods industries will ultimately make possible a very rapid expansion of the supply of consumer goods. (The logic of this argument will be considered in chapter 4.)

To return to the definition of development, a further problem arises.[2] If one speaks of people becoming better off, what does one mean by 'people'. Must development imply that everyone becomes better off and to the same degree? Economic development seems invariably to have benefited people very unequally.

In England during the period 1815–50, a period of exceptionally rapid development, a small minority made fortunes, some who had skills that were in particularly short supply to the fast-growing industries enjoyed a rising standard of living, but for the great majority command over goods and services probably altered very little and this at a time when many of them had their lives badly disrupted by social change. In Uganda, during the years 1945–60, a period of rapidly rising incomes brought about largely by favourable prices of primary products, the benefits were both more immediate and more widespread, because they accrued to the host of cultivators of small farms in the central part of the country. But in areas further away from the railhead, it still did not pay to grow crops for export and consequently inequality in Uganda came to take the form of a growing regional disparity of income. Regional disparities are indeed a characteristic of virtually all but the most highly developed countries. At its simplest this is because development has to begin *somewhere* and it takes time before it can possibly pervade the whole economy.

Another way to illustrate the importance of distribution is to compare pre-independence Kenya with Uganda. Average incomes per head of population were about the same, but the standard of life of Africans in Uganda was incomparably higher because in Kenya so much more of total income accrued to the European settlers and to expatriate businesses.

Enough has been said to indicate that there can be no simple definition of development, so it is best to use one which accords most closely with what most people think it means. In this book economic development will be taken to mean 'a process which makes people in general better off by increasing

2. This is debated in Arthur J. Taylor, *The Standard of Living in Britain in the Industrial Revolution*, Methuen, 1975.

their command over goods and services and by increasing the choices open to them'. This is virtually synonymous with saying that economic development means a rise in the standard of life in the not too distant future. This definition has certain implications that one has simply to swallow in order to escape from endless terminological squabbles. It means, for instance, that if output increases no more rapidly than the growth of population – 2 per cent or more in many underdeveloped countries – or if the whole of an increase in output is devoted to building up a country's military strength or putting up monumental public buildings with which to impress the population and foreign visitors, then that is not economic development. But there is another implication that has only come to be recognized quite recently and that is that if the growth of output is very unevenly distributed so that only a very small minority gain from it, then it does not accord with commonsense to say that a country's standard of life has risen. This reservation is important in the light of a tendency to sponsor development by very capital intensive methods which may not bring about much increase in employment and which therefore may make the distribution of income more unequal. Since most low income countries find that their labour force is now increasing at roughly the same rate as their population as a whole (2–3 per cent p.a.), the failure of employment to increase even though Gross National Product is rising causes even more disguised and open unemployment, and means that increasing numbers have no share at all in the rising standard of living.

The commonest way to assess development is, of course, by reference to a country's Gross National Product. By this standard the underdeveloped countries have made greater progress during the past two decades than many had predicted. The average annual growth in all the underdeveloped countries between 1950 and 1967 was 4·8 per cent. But since their populations increased on average by 2·5 per cent per annum this reduces the average annual growth *per head* to 2·3 per cent (Pearson Report, 1969, chapter 2). Needless to say, these averages conceal wide variation. In Thailand, Syria and Hong Kong GNP increased by 7 per cent p.a. or more whilst in Burma, Ghana and Argentina it was under 3 per cent.

Countries are often ranked according to their total GNP, and their GNP per head of population. The United States has both the largest total GNP and the highest GNP per head of population ($3980). Most Western European countries are estimated to have per capita products of $1500–$2500 per year. At the other end of the spectrum there are thirty-eight countries with populations in excess of one million inhabitants whose GNP per head is $150 or less and another forty-three where it is between $151–$500. In addition there are seventy countries with populations of under one million inhabitants most of which have low incomes by Western European standards, although there are exceptions like Luxemburg and, for different reasons, Kuwait. India and Pakistan, two of the largest countries, are estimated to have *per capita* incomes of $100 (IBRD, 1970).

International comparisons of GNP per head provide rough guidelines of relative welfare but the measure is very rough indeed. The first difficulty is that the national products of different countries are expressed in different currencies having different purchasing power both in international trade and at home.

Since they are expressed in a common currency this has usually involved a conversion at the official rate of exchange. But at best these exchange rates reflect only the price relations of goods entering into international trade. In practice they frequently diverge substantially even from this, since currencies are often over- or under-valued. A further problem arises in that foreign exchange rates cannot be used to measure the relative prices of goods and services that do not enter international trade, for example, housing or personal services. With regard to such goods and services a currency may have a totally different purchasing power from that which it may have over foreign goods. Another difficulty arises from the fact that self-consumed production is a rather large component of total production in underdeveloped countries whilst it is relatively unimportant in the fully monetized high income countries. Since the valuation of self-consumed production is largely arbitrary the published statistics of GNP of an under-developed country are much affected by the method of valuation of this component. Finally, it is also arguable that the national products especially of very dissimilar countries are made up of totally different goods and services and satisfy equally different 'needs' determined by different climatic conditions and institutional factors. For example, the income of a given Indian sustains him and his family in India, but converted into dollars would not provide him with enough food, clothes and shelter to stay alive in America. On the other hand, the suggestion that Indians have less need for heating and therefore do not need so large an income has sometimes invited the rejoinder that their 'need' for air conditioning may be greater. Enough has been said to draw attention to some of the difficulties that arise in the too ready resort to international comparisons of GNP, but nothing that has been said can affect the conclusion that differences of the order of magnitude quoted earlier give *some* indication of the existing real differences in welfare that exist between countries.

Although GNP per head is still the best *single* indicator of differences in the standard of life between countries it could and should be supplemented by others. For example, despite the great steps forward in reducing mortality that have been taken since the Second World War the average expectation of life at birth is still only forty-eight years in the low income countries, whereas in developed countries it is seventy. Energy consumption per head in the low income countries is the equivalent of 275 kilogrammes of coal compared with 5050 kgms in the developed countries as a whole and 9200 kgms in the United States, reflecting perhaps better than any other indicator the disparity in the degree of industrial development. Average literacy is reckoned to be 38 per cent in the under-developed countries as compared to 96 per cent in the developed countries (Meier, 1970, pp. 21–2).

Considering how often one hears it said that 'two thirds of the world are hungry' it is worth pointing out that the disparities in daily calorie intake between underdeveloped and developed countries is not nearly so great as these other indicators – 2250 compared to 2920. But this hides large differences in the quality of the food consumed. In the high income countries much of the food intake is in the form of meat, fish, dairy produce, vegetables and fruit which provide a nutritious, balanced diet, whilst in the poor countries diets are predominantly starchy so that an apparently satisfactory calorie intake is not incompatible with widespread deficiencies of protein and essential vitamins.

The starkest differences appear in the provision of durable consumer goods. For example, in 1965 there were 0·5 passenger motor vehicles for every 100 of the population in the underdeveloped countries: in the developed countries the comparable figure was twenty-one and in the United States alone, thirty-eight (Meier, 1970, p. 22).

Such piecemeal comparisons are, of course, less easy to use than aggregate national income statistics and this has led to a number of attempts to find some more satisfactory aggregate measure of comparison. The most notable is that of Professor W. Beckerman (1966) using non-monetary indicators such as steel consumption, cement production, the number of letters sent, the stock of radio receivers, of telephones, of motor vehicles and the consumption of meat as 'explanatory variables' to predict real per capita consumption. Figures produced on this basis yield rather different comparative estimates of real per capita consumption than statistics of GNP (Beckerman, 1966, pp. 36–7) though they do not affect the broad grouping of countries according to their level of development.

We now return to a description of some of the salient features of low income countries. One such characteristic is the low level of accumulated capital. One reason why advanced industrial countries enjoy high standards of living is that production is aided by a large stock of machines, and overhead capital that have accumulated over long periods of time. Thus in Great Britain the total capital stock including domestic buildings and other items that have not much to do with productivity is estimated at some £100,000 million, or roughly two and a half times the GNP. In most underdeveloped countries the capital stock, even on the most generous computations is more likely to be a fraction – and a small one at that – than a multiple of GNP.

It is, however, a mistake to explain differences in productivity and the standard of living solely in terms of differences in the stock of accumulated capital. One must also look at natural resources and the skill and knowledge of a population in making the most of their natural resources. The skill in exploiting resources is especially important. Professor Francis L. K. Hsu, an anthropologist, points out that when the American Indians first came to the New World twenty thousand years ago they found it as laden with mineral wealth as did the Pilgrims much later. The American Indians exploited little of these resources.

Many European peoples on the other hand, went to far corners of the earth looking for what they wanted when they failed to find it at home. The availability of the resources did nothing to encourage the former, whilst their absence did not discourage the latter (Hsu, 1954, p. 323).

Hsu attributes these differences to 'the factor of culture'. Another example of differences in skill and knowledge is provided by rice which has long been grown in a number of tropical countries; but the yield per acre varies greatly as the following figures show:

Kilograms of rice (paddy) per hectare, 1964–5

Japan	5200
India	1600
Australia	6100

Source: *FAO* (1964).

Some of these differences are due to variations in the amounts of physical capital used in production, and Japan uses about four times as much labour per hectare as India on farms that are on average a third of the size of India's. But the most important part of the explanation for the observed differences in output per hectare is the difference in skill of the farmers and this in turn is partly explicable in terms of what is described as human capital produced by education. Capital embodied in people does not appear in statistics of a country's capital stock and yet it may be that this is quantitatively the most important part of a country's capital stock. The reason why Germany was rebuilt so quickly after the Second World War when much of its physical capital stock had been destroyed by air raids was in part that the skill and knowledge of Germans had remained intact.

Small though the capital stock of low income countries may be, it is certain to be bigger than most official estimates. The official figures often underestimate capital formation because they are based on imported capital goods. These imports are taken as the basic figure to which a margin is then added, as also a separate estimate for construction. Since the currencies of many underdeveloped countries are overvalued this gives a systematic understatement of the figures of capital formation. Richard W. Hooley who studied capital formation in nineteen countries found that the exchange rate was overvalued in sixteen of them at some time during the preceding decade; in nine of them the overvaluation was 100 per cent or more (Hooley, 1967). The official estimates also often omit important components of capital formation. For example, they leave out privately built dams, minor roads, farm irrigation or land clearing. They seldom include small farm improvements such as putting a corrugated iron roof on a grain store, or building a concrete slab on which to dry coffee; and yet such forms of investment are vital in raising agricultural productivity. Another item likely to be excluded is the bicycle because in the countries where national income accounting was first developed a bicycle is a durable consumer good, not a capital good. But in peasant economies it is often the principal means of access to the market. The reason why the heavily built 'old-fashioned' bicycle remains so popular is that it is used to carry heavy loads of plantains or cotton on the back. It has been much more difficult to develop cash crop farming in Western Uganda precisely because it is too hilly there to use a bicycle.

What applies to the capital stock applies equally to capital formation or the process of creating the capital stock, viz. that official figures tend to leave out some forms of capital formation. This does not necessarily matter provided one remembers that one must not then expect to find some neat relationship between capital formation and the growth of output, such as a stable incremental capital output ratio.[3] Recent research in the West has shown that only part of the growth there during this century is explicable by reference to increases in capital and labour and that the 'residual' is to be attributed to improvements in the *quality* of the factors of production and especially labour. The resulting rise in the productivity of labour is in turn attributed to education, so that one should really treat at least a part of a country's expenditure on education as investment (in human capital). Yet the uniform statistical convention in all countries has always been to treat, for example, government expenditure on the salaries of teachers, or agricultural extension workers, as recurrent expenditure and it therefore figures in the national income accounts as 'public authorities' expenditure on currently produced goods and services'. Even though saving in the underdeveloped countries is estimated by the Pearson Report to have been 15 per cent of GNP between 1960–67, countries are sometimes taken to task by foreign aid donors for failing to devote enough of their resources to capital formation (Pearson Report, 1969, p. 31). Such strictures invariably ignore great increases in expenditure on education and health services and indeed countries are often accused of spending too much on education. Such criticism is legitimate if expenditure is on the wrong sort of education, or if it is excessive in relation to complementary outlays needed to enable the educated to use their education. But some part of educational expenditure is likely to have effects on output which are directly comparable to investment in physical capital (Balogh and Streeten, 1963).

Whilst some argue that a country is failing to 'save' enough

3. How widely they range is neatly illustrated by Table 60 in UN Industrial Development Organization, 1969.

of its income, others say that low incomes set a ceiling to the capacity to save and make elaborate calculations to show by how much domestic savings need to be augmented with Foreign Aid to ensure some target rate of growth. In practice countries probably have a good deal of leeway in how much they devote to capital formation. As Professor Hirschman (1958) has pointed out, determined rulers have in all ages succeeded in devoting to capital formation as high a proportion of total resources as any country now succeeds in mobilizing, as witness the pyramids of Egypt, the temples of Bangkok or the cathedrals of medieval Europe! The difference is that these were non-productive ventures – at least, as ordinarily understood – but if there is a strong will to develop in a country, a high rate of productive capital accumulation should be no more difficult. Indeed the rate of saving in many countries *is* high, but it does not lead to productive capital formation because it is hoarded in non-productive forms: cattle in Africa used as a store of value not a factor of production; precious metal and stones in South East Asia. Nor are sacrifices to propitiate the Gods necessarily a productive form of capital formation!

If people save but do not invest it is not because they are anti-social or bloody-minded, but rather because another characteristic feature of low income countries is that there is either a notable lack of investment opportunities or else there is an equally notable failure to perceive them. Part of the task of development must always be to locate avenues of investment that lead to a growth of output. Entrepreneurial talent or a knowledge of what other countries have achieved in similar circumstances are just as important as the availability of capital. Historically, capital accumulation of the productive sort has probably been the *result* of a widening of markets or technical innovation rather than the cause of it. It is when, for some reason, new opportunities for investment occur or are perceived that the resources needed to exploit them are harnessed. And that is as true of the Soviet Union in the 1920s as of England in the eighteenth century.

Many underdeveloped countries especially in Latin America

have experienced rapid inflation in the course of development. Between 1963–71 the general level of prices increased more than eleven-fold in Brazil, nearly eight fold in Chile and four-fold in Argentina. By comparison British prices rose by 32 per cent and those of Germany 12 per cent (UN, 1971).

There is much disagreement as to the cause of such inflation. One school – 'the monetarists' – attributes the inflation to the monetary policies pursued by governments. They allege that governments have been afraid to levy taxes or to curb expenditure and that inflation is the direct result of excessive money creation to finance public development expenditure. Others, the 'structuralists', see inflation rather as the result of imbalance between industrial development and the food supply. They argue that the failure to augment the food supply to keep pace with a rising urban demand causes food prices to rise. The resulting rise in the urban cost of living then causes industrial wages and prices to rise. The structuralists regard the undeniable increase in the money supply as a symptom, not a cause, of an inflation that has its real root in the inelasticity of supply of a backward and stagnant agriculture (Kindleberger, 1965, ch. 13; Felix and Grunwalds chapters in Hirschman (ed.), 1961; Ellis and Wallich (eds.), 1961).

Finally, it is a salient characteristic of poor countries that many exhibit marked regional inequalities. The reason is, of course, fundamentally, that development has to start somewhere and that it takes time for it to spread. But there is evidence that in the absence of positive steps to ensure the spread of development there may be forces tending towards ever greater regional inequality. Italy is often cited as a country in which the rapid industrial development in the North has not spread to the South and where even the most Herculean attempts to promote development in the so-called *Mezzogiorno* in the last twenty years have failed to make a major contribution to narrowing the gap. Economics is deeply imbued with the idea of the swinging pendulum that eventually – in equilibrium – comes to rest. Gunnar Myrdal has argued that in social processes what he calls 'circular cumulative causation' is more often the normal case and that it is rare for a system to move towards any sort of balance between opposing forces.

'In the normal case', he writes, 'a change does not call forth countervailing changes but, instead, supporting changes, which move the system in the same direction as the first change but much further. Because of such circular causation a social process tends to become cumulative and often to gather speed at an accelerating rate' (Myrdal, 1963, p. 13).

This idea can be applied to regional inequality: development in one region does not necessarily have the effect of stimulating development in neighbouring regions, but on the contrary leads often to a 'backwash' on these regions making them poorer than ever. External economies in the growing regions, including social overhead capital such as roads, schools, hospitals, and supplies of piped water and electricity, far outweigh any advantages that the poor regions might offer, such as a cheaper supply of labour. The backwash effect can be even greater if labour moves to the growing regions. It often happens that it is the young, the most able and most enterprising who move, thus leaving backward regions with the elderly and the less able. Sometimes the backward regions may even be impoverished by the destruction of handicrafts in the face of competition from factory-produced goods in the developing region.

Myrdal's analysis is persuasive up to a point and it is not difficult to find illustrations of the phenomena he analyses. Only active Government intervention to counteract these tendencies can, according to him, ensure evenly spread development, and Myrdal maintains that the few developed countries which have become largely integrated internally owe this to State action helping poor people and depressed industries and areas.

Probably Myrdal's gloom is overdone. New industries or other new economic activities have often gone to new locations because they possessed hitherto unimportant natural resources. Thus the industrial revolution of eighteenth century England had its cradle not in the South which was the most advanced part of the country, but in the totally undeveloped North because that was where first waterpower and later coal needed for steampower and iron smelting were to be found. Recently the rapid growth of tourism in a number of underdeveloped countries has opened up new locations of economic activity.

One could of course continue *ad infinitum* to elaborate characteristics which distinguish low income economies from those at the other end of the spectrum. For example in low income countries very few earn their livelihood by working for wages; the overwhelming majority are members of a peasant family household and wage earners rarely account for more than 10 per cent of the labour force. Women are generally an important part of the labour force; often, especially in Africa, they do much of the routine work in the fields. A sizeable part of total farm production is for self-consumption, or subsistence, rather than for sale, in contrast with the countries of Western Europe where a little vegetable growing in the back garden or home-decorating form only a very minor part of total economic activity.

But having said something about characteristics which underdeveloped countries have in common, one must also stress again their great diversity and, especially, the diversity of the development problems they face. It does not make good sense to treat the problems of small island economies in the Pacific or Caribbean as if they were the same as India's, with her population of over 500 million. Arguments that might be adduced in support of the development of basic industries in India clearly would make no sense at all when applied to, say, Tonga or the British Virgin Islands – the latter with a population of some 10,000. This is worth remembering later when we shall consider some universal strategies that have been sometimes advocated, for example, a strategy of pursuing balanced growth, or of giving priority to industrial growth. Policies need to be as varied as the countries to which they are to be applied. Industrial growth has no magic power that makes it invariably superior to growth via tourist development or market gardening both of which have been highly successful in raising incomes in Kenya and elsewhere. Given the very high income elasticity of demand for holiday travel in Western Europe, America and Australia, and falling air fares, the potential for countries that are attractive to tourists is very large. Tourist arrivals in East Africa increased by 18 per cent a year between 1961 and 1967 and totalled 150,000 in the latter year (Mitchell, 1970). In some of the small island countries the relative impact on the economy of rapid tourist development has been far greater.

Countries also differ greatly in their resource endowments and this can have a crucial bearing upon their ability to export. The example usually given is that of the oil producing countries of the Middle East, which differ critically from most other underdeveloped countries in that they have an ample supply of foreign exchange and also have no shortage of resources for development. The development problem in these countries is quite different: the oil revenues permit an immediate and very large improvement in the standard of life for all. The development problem is how to channel some of the revenues into other productive assets and into raising educational standards. But oil is only the most spectacular example of a resource only to be found in a few places and which gives those who have it an *absolute* advantage in international trade. More commonly, countries have to be content to avail themselves of comparative advantages. Market gardening in Kenya, to serve both the Nairobi and London markets, is an example of seizing a comparative advantage that few other underdeveloped countries possess. Kenya's climate and soil lend themselves to temperate zone vegetable growing and Kenya farmers took advantage of very low air freights to ship their produce to Covent Garden. The air carriers had often returned empty from Nairobi and were therefore prepared to quote low rates which made Kenya vegetable prices very competitive. It is precisely the differences in size, in resource endowments, in the aptitudes of their inhabitants and in their geographical position which make the problem of development more manageable than it would be if all were alike.

2 Explanations of Low Incomes

The most widely canvassed notion seeking to explain why countries have failed to develop is that they are trapped in a series of interlocking vicious circles of poverty and stagnation. The circles take poverty as their starting point. The first shows that poverty means low productivity and low incomes; these lead to low savings and thus to low levels of investment. The low level of investment in turn perpetuates a deficiency of capital which then explains continued poverty. This vicious circle therefore emphasizes the role of saving in development and seeks to demonstrate that low savings are both a cause and effect of the initial poverty.

Another 'vicious circle' is said to be that the existing low incomes are insufficient to provide the peoples' minimum nutritional requirements and that this impairs their physical efficiency thus reducing their productivity and perpetuating the low incomes which were the initial cause.

Yet another circle emphasizes the role of demand in development. Poverty implies a low level of aggregate demand which then in turn explains why there is a dearth of profitable investment opportunities, and therefore very little investment. In this way, too, the deficiency of capital which is said to be the root of poverty is perpetuated. In other words this thesis claims, to quote P. T. Bauer, one of its most trenchant critics, 'that poverty itself sets up well nigh insurmountable obstacles to its own conquest' (Bauer, 1965).

It is an attractively simple notion, intuitively plausible but almost totally erroneous. It was given much currency by the late Professor Nurkse in one of the earliest books on under-developed countries (Nurkse, 1953). Nurkse used the idea of interlocking vicious circles in support of his thesis that the only way to promote development was to break into the vicious circle by capital investment from abroad or by foreign aid. With an injection of capital, productivity would rise and the resulting higher incomes would eventually generate higher savings, sufficient to carry on the momentum of capital formation initially created by the injection of capital from abroad. Higher incomes would then also increase aggregate demand and so give further impetus to capital formation by creating profitable investment opportunities.

If this thesis were valid it would be difficult to explain the existence today of many developed countries which started with low incomes per head and low stocks of accumulated capital, and which indeed exhibited many of the features of today's underdeveloped countries. Yet many of these countries developed without appreciable injections of outside capital, and certainly without foreign aid. Foreign aid and private investment have, of course, sometimes made important contributions to economic advance in recent years – Taiwan and Puerto Rico are conspicuous examples – but they are neither a necessary nor sufficient condition of development, and it is indeed important to stress that simple mechanistic models of development do little to explain the complex social, cultural and economic processes which bring about the development of economies. They also provide little guidance for the pursuit of sensible policies. For example, the vicious circle thesis implies a model in which saving is a function of income and income or output are in turn functionally related to capital formation. We shall argue later (chapter 4) that growth models based on unvarying capital output ratios are often misleading. Here we need only stress that economic development in all countries has usually been associated with great disruptions of these functional relationships. Even the poorest small cultivators are suddenly found to command the resources for adding a cash crop to their production if this appears to promise a substantial rise in their standard of life.

A second economic explanation of underdevelopment has been offered by Myrdal (1963). He argues that the very process of development in one part of the world has had the effect of impoverishing other parts, or at any rate made it more difficult for them to develop. He refers to this effect as 'backwash'. Most economists had argued that development in one part of the world would create 'spread effects' for the rest, i.e. that the benefits of development would spread by increasing the demand for imports and creating additional supplies of capital for foreign investment. Classical economic theory had led one to expect that international trade based on comparative advantage would ensure that the benefits of it were spread, and that the free movement of goods and of capital and labour would prevent anything more than a momentary advantage from being perpetuated. Economic theory thus seemed to rule out the possibility of more than temporary inequality between countries. International inequality could therefore persist only if the market mechanism was prevented from functioning freely, in much the same way as it was commonly argued in the days before Keynes that persistent unemployment could only be explained by reference to interference with competition in the labour market on the part of trade unions, which prevented downward flexibility of wages.

Some formulations of the classical doctrine did not require movements of capital and labour between countries to bring about the equalization of factor prices and therefore of earnings and incomes. During the nineteenth century the theory seemed to work, in the sense that the development of North America and Australia seemed to support it. But the twentieth century has been characterized by ever greater inequalities between nations and it is becoming increasingly difficult to explain these differences as purely the result of restrictions on international trade. The fact of restrictions is not in dispute, nor need one deny that if underdeveloped countries were given unimpeded access to the markets of the advanced industrial countries this would help to raise their incomes. But it is difficult to believe that free trade would by itself be sufficient to eliminate the enormous inequalities between the poor countries and the rich. That is why the classical theory of international trade is not in itself sufficient to explain persistent inequality. Myrdal, however, goes further and argues that in the absence of counteracting measures, trade will not move *towards* the equalization of incomes, but on the contrary make the differences ever greater. He argues that a widening of markets often

strengthens the rich and progressive countries whose manufacturing industries have the lead and are already fortified by the surrounding external economies while the underdeveloped countries are in continuous danger of seeing even what they have of industry and, in particular, small scale industry and handicrafts priced out by cheap imports from industrial countries (Myrdal, 1963, p. 51).

The main positive effect of international trade, he continues, has been to promote the production of primary products, employing mostly unskilled labour. Since primary products often meet inelastic demands in the export markets they do little to promote development. On the contrary trade tends only to have backwash effects and 'to strengthen the forces maintaining stagnation or regression' (Myrdal, 1963). Nor can one rely on capital movements to counteract international inequality. Capital will shun the underdeveloped countries because it can earn higher returns in the 'advanced' countries. In contrast to these strong backwash effects the 'spread' effects of international economic relations are very weak (Myrdal, 1963, p. 54).

Persuasive though this analysis may be it suffers from one great defect: it fails to explain the very remarkable development which has in fact occurred in many underdeveloped countries. Poverty is compatible with even rapid advance if this is of recent origin and began from a low level. To use Professor P. T. Bauer's apt words, one must beware of confusing 'a low economic level with a zero rate of change' (Bauer, 1959, p. 108). The great progress which has taken place in many underdeveloped regions since the beginning of this century is at least as remarkable as the disparity that still remains between rich and poor countries. One has only to remember the growth of the great cocoa-growing industry in Ghana or the very recent industrial development of Hong Kong both of which have brought their inhabitants very marked increases in income even if these incomes are still low by the standards of the 'advanced' countries. The thesis of backwash is also refuted by the fact that if it had universal validity it would be difficult to explain why once any one country had developed others could ever have developed subsequently. If one took the thesis literally 'there would for centuries past have been only one developed country constantly increasing its lead over the others' (Bauer, 1959, p. 109).

Some explanations of the level of incomes found in many countries outside North America and Europe can be considered more briefly. One such explanation focuses attention on the density of population. It is argued that development is made difficult by the high density of population. This can be readily conceded provided it is remembered that this is perhaps especially an Asian problem and that there is no 'overpopulation' in many parts of Latin America or Africa even though average incomes there may be just as low. Many of the countries of South East Asia that are densely populated now also started initially with sparse populations in relation to their natural resources, so that 'overpopulation' cannot be used as an explanation of the present low levels of income. We also know that high population density is not especially a feature of low income countries but is found equally in some of the richest like Great Britain.

Others have attributed the low level of development either to colonial exploitation, or to the deliberate and legalized political, economic and racial discrimination imposed by advanced countries on peoples who could not defend themselves. Although this has been an important factor in many countries here again, to quote Professor H. Myint, 'it does not explain why the indigenous peoples of other countries who are not subject to such obvious discriminations to the same extent should also be similarly backward' (Myint, 1954). It is equally possible to argue that colonial governments have in their time established internal peace, efficient government, basic infrastructure facilities such as roads, railways and ports and in other ways created the conditions for progress on which Adam Smith in the eighteenth century laid so much stress. There have certainly been a number of instances in the past decade where the breakdown of internal peace has had disastrous effects on production and a large scale reversion to subsistence conditions – both in the sense of the minimum needed for survival and of production for self-consumption – because of the breakdown of markets in which goods were formerly sold.

The preceding paragraphs have poured cold water on some of the more sweeping explanations why countries have low incomes. It would, however, be wrong to dismiss them out of hand, just because each can be shown not to hold in some particular country or at some particular time. Each contains an insight which, even if it does not provide a universal explanation may be helpful in understanding some particular instance of retarded development. Were it otherwise, one would hardly have been justified in discussing it.

Non-economic explanations for low incomes

It must of course be immediately apparent that whilst economic factors determine the outcome of development, the process itself cannot be explicable in economic terms alone. What is more difficult is to assess the relative roles played by social, cultural, historical and psychological factors, and no attempt will be made here to do so, let alone to adjudicate between rival theories. It is however reasonable to point out that there do seem to exist greatly varying propensities to develop among different peoples at any one time, and that these may be more easily explicable in non-economic terms. Development depends on having people who are enterprising. Frequently – but not invariably – an initial upsurge of development is attributable to the enterprise exhibited by some minority group in a population – Chinese in South East Asia, 'Levantines' in West Africa, Asians in East Africa, Parsees in India, samurai in nineteenth century Japan, or Non Conformists in seventeenth century England. What they share is neither a common race nor a particular set of beliefs that might predispose them to entrepreneurial aptitudes. They do however have in common minority status or 'deviance' and perhaps the resulting feelings of insecurity propel them forward towards seeking economic success in a way that distinguishes them from the rest (cf. Hoselitz, 1957, p. 35).

Professor David C. McClelland has attempted to establish that the 'need to achieve' is present to very varying degrees in different populations and that there is a clear association between a country's rate of economic development and the amount of achievement motivation found when psychological tests were applied to groups of school children in that country (McClelland, 1961).[1] Professor Everett Hagen places more emphasis on the effect of early childhood training on the formation of personality. He maintains that economic development is hardly possible so long as small children are brought up in a very authoritarian way. This inculcates attitudes inimical to economic development which become part of the personality and are thus passed on from generation to generation, perpetuating what he calls a traditional society. These trammels are shaken off only when society's respect has been withdrawn from some substantial group of men who have consequently become passive and apathetic. Their wives then react by applauding and encouraging activity among their young instead of constantly seeking to protect and restrain them. In this way a generation of potential entrepreneurs comes into being who play a major role in their country's economic development (Hagen, 1964).[2] Hagen provides a wealth of illustrations from history and the four corners of the earth, but his evidence is far from conclusive. To link the English Industrial Revolution of the eighteenth century to events eight centuries earlier, as he does, would seem to require evidence which simply does not exist. Nor is the importance he attaches to child rearing altogether convincing. As Gerschenkron points out, child training in Germany before the First World War probably resembled very closely what Hagen quotes to be the situation in present day Burma; yet their paths of development have been markedly dissimilar. Hagen claims that his theory has considerable predictive

1. For a very critical discussion see Schatz (1965).

2. For a fuller account and trenchant critique see Gerschenkron, 1968 (pp. 368–74).

value, but if one does not know whether the predicted change is likely to occur in one generation or eight centuries, this must detract from the theory's immediate usefulness. This is not to deny however, that non-economic phenomena may not be just as important as economic ones in explaining economic development and the sociologists' writings on the role of deviants and minorities seem well substantiated.

It has often been argued that the real explanation for underdevelopment is that the social systems and cultures of the low income countries are not adaptable to economic change. One of the earliest exponents of this view is Boeke who based much of his analysis upon Dutch experience in Indonesia (Boeke, 1953). According to Boeke capitalistic methods of production and distribution fail to spread from export industries established and directed by Western entrepreneurs, because of the absence of the cultural and social prerequisites for Western capitalism. Western economies are based upon unlimited wants, a money economy and large scale organization. Boeke claims that people in South East Asia have only limited wants and that therefore their supply curve of effort is backward sloping. Labour fails to respond positively to stimuli intended to enhance output. Small-scale producers who dominate production likewise are not profit-oriented and can neither be induced to increase output by the offer of higher prices nor are they willing to assume the risks of adopting better techniques of production introduced from advanced Western countries. Production is organized on the basis of the extended family and exchange is confined to neighbourhood barter.

. . . anyone expecting Western reactions will meet with frequent surprises. When the price of coconut is high, the chances are that less of the commodities will be offered for sale; when wages are raised the manager of the estate risks that less work will be done; if three acres are enough to supply the needs of the household a cultivator will not till six; when rubber prices fall the owner of a grove may decide to tap more intensively, whereas high prices may mean that he leaves a larger or smaller portion of tappable trees untapped (Boeke, 1953, p. 40).

In short, Boeke's explanation for the failure of modern economic techniques to spread from the export sector to other parts of the economy is simply that 'the basic values and attitudes of the indigenous population are incompatible with the type of behaviour required to introduce and successfully maintain production based on the advanced techniques of developed economies' (Baldwin, 1966, p. 7).

This gives rise to dual societies in which an imported social system co-exists with an indigenous social system, unable to oust or supersede it. Put in a different way it leads to the existence of 'enclave economies' or areas of economic activity within the underdeveloped countries which are governed by the techniques, motivations and organization of advanced Western economies, whilst the indigenous economic activities remain unaffected. This condition is often referred to as 'dualism', and according to Boeke, Western economic theory is totally inapplicable to 'dualistic' economies. Boeke's view of the prospects for economic development is one of extreme pessimism. If he was unique in holding this view one could perhaps dismiss his writings as those of a gloomy crank, but in practice his view was at one time widely shared especially among colonial administrators and it continues to be voiced by Western businessmen operating in underdeveloped countries.

In discussing the assertion that people in underdeveloped countries have limited wants one must distinguish clearly between the statement that they can think of no satisfactory way of spending increases in income and the statement that they see no simple way of raising their standard of living by their own efforts or enterprise. The former is manifestly untrue. Villagers everywhere have shown an eagerness to spend windfall increases in their income, resulting perhaps from a sudden rise in export prices of cash crops, on a wide range of imported consumer goods. When they have abstained from increased consumption it has been because they saw in the windfall an opportunity to increase the productivity of their farms by engaging in capital formation. The latter statement is more plausible but is by no means confined to underdeveloped countries. It tends to be a phenomenon associated with any society which has stagnated or slowed down long enough 'to weaken the "demonstration effect" provided by people moving from one standard of living to another as the result of their own extra effort directed specifically towards earning additional income' (Higgins, 1956, p. 108). It is also often true that social pressures weigh down on those who try to break out of the accustomed standard of life; this is particularly so in villages as distinct from the more anonymous towns. It occurs, typically, in situations in which people see no prospect of rising to a higher level of living by making greater efforts. The British coal industry after the Second World War provides an interesting example. It was observed in a period of labour shortage that every wage increase intended to attract more workers to the industry and to enhance the pay of those already in it, led only to more absences from work. Coal miners live in pit villages each under the close scrutiny of his neighbours. There was a set pattern of life and of expenditure and hostility towards anyone trying to break away from it and who tried to rise above the customary level of living. If a miner were to buy a car or a washing machine he would make himself unpopular at best and a laughing-stock at worst. Consequently there was no point in earning more than was necessary to maintain the customary standard of life. But what has to be remembered is that ultimately these social sanctions give way. Gradually, as working people in other parts of England took the opportunity to attain a higher standard of life than had seemed possible before the War, so gradually the pressures towards conformity were eroded and miners, too, started to acquire a range of durable consumer goods much beyond the previously approved level, as wages continued to rise and the fear of unemployment receded.

But the notion of the backward bending supply curve of effort calls for closer scrutiny. In the last ten to fifteen years it has been largely discredited as one example after another showed that what appeared to be an unnaturally high leisure preference, turned out, on closer investigation, to be explained in a quite different way. For example, it was said of Ugandan farmers in the late 1940s and early 1950s that despite substantial increases in the price of cotton, growers reduced rather than increased their production. What was ignored was that at this time coffee growing was becoming much more profitable and that far from being irrational the growers switched to coffee because it promised to yield a much higher return than cotton, at almost any probable ratio of coffee to cotton prices. Further, the yield from coffee was spread over a greater part of the year than cotton which had all to be harvested and sold at once. Another example from Uganda relates to factory wage earners. Absenteeism was regarded as altogether excessive and was attributed to limited wants. Investigation revealed that many of the absentees used the day off to take on some much more highly paid temporary casual work, or to hawk round a load of fish or vegetables sent to them by relatives from their village. Even to attend a deceased relative's funeral may yield a much higher reward than the day's wage foregone in the factory. What was generally attributed to high leisure preference or limited wants turned out to have an opposite explanation (Elkan, 1960). In the former Belgian Congo it was reported that farmers would not apply manure to their manioc and beans although on a demonstration plot nearby they could easily see for themselves that the application of manure resulted in a more than five-fold increase in their yields. What was particularly puzzling was that they were quite prepared to apply manure to their banana trees. Investigation revealed that it had to do with the prevailing system of land tenure. According to customary law, the ownership of the land is vested in the Chief; and while the tenant enjoys permanent tenure in respect of land on which permanent crops like bananas are grown, he has no permanent tenure in respect of land on which he can only grow annual crops like manioc or beans. This being so, farmers were very reluctant to increase the yield on an annual crop lest they be deprived of their land by a covetous Chief. Here we have an example of perfectly rational economic behaviour once the social constraints are properly understood (Neumark, 1958).

In many parts of Africa the fact that workers on plantations or in the towns returned after a few years to their villages was taken as evidence of limited wants. What escaped notice was that this, too, was rational, maximizing, behaviour. Wage employment provided young men with the best opportunity to accumulate savings with which to turn a subsistence farm into one yielding a cash income. In the long run, the prospective yield from cash crop farming was higher than from wage employment until the 1960s, and we find here again how what appeared irrational on the surface turned out to be quite rational economic behaviour when viewed from the vantage point of the people concerned.

Finally, farmers are often accused of being conservative because they will not immediately try out every new technique suggested to them. What tends to be forgotten is that many farmers exist at the margin of subsistence where it may be more rational to minimize risks than to maximize yields. A new technique may indeed promise a substantial increase in yield. But if its adoption entails any risk at all that in a bad year the new technique may lead to a total harvest failure, then this is a risk which no poor small-scale cultivator will be prepared to take (Lipton, 1968). This helps to explain why, as will appear in chapter 7, it has been the larger, more prosperous farmers in India and Pakistan, who have been the first to take advantage of the new dwarf varieties of wheat and rice that have wrought the so-called 'Green Revolution'. They have been more progressive, to quote Galbraith, not because of their higher intelligence, but because of their higher incomes (Galbraith, 1965, p. 3).

3 Trade and Development

Nineteenth century experience has shown that international trade can make an impressive contribution to a country's economic development. This contribution is usually portrayed as deriving in part from the 'static' or direct gains from trade, and in part from the 'dynamic' or indirect gains. These terms need explanation: assume that a country has a given endowment of resources and that they are all fully employed. Trade theory then shows that by reallocating resources so as to increase the production of goods in which the country has a comparative advantage, trade will procure for it a greater total volume of goods than could have been obtained directly. By moving along its production possibility boundary and engaging in trade, a country can 'consume' a combination of goods greater than it could 'produce', or in other words its consumption position will lie outside its production possibility boundary.[1] The size of these static gains will depend on the rate of exchange; indeed, trade will take place only if the rate of exchange is such as to produce gains, so that in the extreme one could conceive of a situation in which even though a country had a comparative advantage in the production of a good, trade would not take place because the rate of exchange nullified any gains that might have been derived from it.

It may also be that a country's resources are initially not fully employed and that international trade opens up the possibility of a 'vent for surplus'. By moving onto its production possibility boundary a country can produce a surplus to exchange for imported goods which it cannot itself produce or for which it has an unsatisfied demand. This, too is a 'static'

1. Production possibility boundaries are briefly explained at the beginning of chapter 4, or more fully in Lipsey (1966, chapter 4).

gain. The export expansion of peasant products, particularly from South East Asia and from Uganda and West Africa took place not so much through the reallocation of given and fully employed resources from the domestic to the export sector, as through bringing hitherto underutilized land and labour in the subsistence economy into export production (Myint, 1971, p. 180).

The 'dynamic' or indirect gains from trade arise from the advantages of specialization which occur as a result of trade. International trade releases a country from the narrowness of domestic markets; greater division of labour will raise the productivity of its resources through the growth of specialized skills and the introduction of specialized techniques and capital equipment in the export sector. It also allows a country to realize economies of scale. The gains from such specialization and economies of scale are 'dynamic' in the sense that in contrast with the static gains, they represent an outward shift of the production possibility boundary in the direction of the goods produced for export. But the gains from increased productivity in the export sector and the rising real incomes they engender are then also said to spread to the rest of the economy, resulting in an 'export-led' growth (Myint, 1971, p. 178). If, as a result of trade, national income rises and the consequent increase in savings lead to productive investment, then the ensuing growth of national income can be viewed as yet a further 'dynamic' gain from international trade.

Thus the theory predicts that international trade can increase welfare partly by moving an economy along or onto its production possibility boundary, and partly by simultaneously moving this boundary outwards.

The classical economists, especially Adam Smith and John Stuart Mill, were very much concerned with the idea of trade as an 'engine of growth'. Thus Mill writing in the middle of the nineteenth century pointed out that in a hitherto isolated country the growth of international trade might make people 'acquainted with new objects' and 'the easier acquisition of things which they had not previously thought attainable, sometimes works a sort of industrial revolution in a country whose resources were previously undeveloped' (Mill, quoted by Meier, 1963).

This is nowadays referred to as the 'international demonstration effect' – except that this concept is more often used to explain impedances to development. It is argued that poor countries have their demands for consumer goods stimulated by being made aware of how people live in richer countries, and that this increases the propensity to consume and therefore reduces potential savings that could be used to increase the stock of capital. Mill viewed it differently, when he emphasized the 'educative effect' of trade; '. . . placing human beings in contact with persons dissimilar from themselves, and with modes of thought and action unlike those with which they are familiar . . . has always been . . . one of the primary sources of progress' (Mill, quoted by Meier, 1963). Foreign trade enables a primary producing country to import machinery and to pay for overseas technical training. The late-nineteenth century history of Japan is perhaps the most spectacular example of trade (the export of raw silk) paying for the transformation of the domestic economy through the import of capital goods and the education and training of Japanese students at European universities and technical colleges.

Myrdal and others have argued that the facts are completely at variance with the predictions of traditional trade theory. They argue that whilst the theory predicts a levelling out of international disparities of income, the fact is that international inequality has become ever greater. It is true that the traditional view may be summarized as being that trade is capable of transmitting development. It can also be shown that under certain restrictive conditions free international trade is a perfect substitute for the complete international mobility of factors and is sufficient to equalize not only the prices of the products being traded but even the prices of the factors of production. This is the case of Samuelson's 'factor-price equalization theorem' which shows that under assumptions which were known to be very restrictive, wages and profits in the countries that trade with each other will tend towards equality (Samuelson 1948). Myrdal has argued that in practice, far from tending towards equality, international trade sets up a cumulative process away from equilibrium in factor prices. This 'cumulative causation' causes a growing disparity of world incomes. Samuelson however never claimed empirical validity for his 'factor-price equalization theorem' and the conventional theory (except in Samuelson's very special case), never claimed that trade would *equalize* real incomes, but only that under certain conditions real incomes would be higher with trade than without trade. Nor is it legitimate to attribute solely to international trade the historical trend towards polarization of countries' incomes. A static theory cannot be refuted with time-series evidence unless all other forces impinging on the world distribution of income can be deemed to have remained constant. This would be an absurd assumption to make and if other variables moved in an adverse direction, a polarization of world incomes need not be incompatible with the classical theory of comparative cost.

Conventional trade theory draws attention to the possible gains from trade. What it does not say is that trade must inevitably bring about gains in welfare and by far the most interesting question is why international trade has not always led to growth or why the growth it has induced has sometimes been confined to a once-for-all shift of the production possibility boundary, instead of being self-sustained and therefore continuous. In this connection the persistence of 'enclaves' of development which fail to spread to the rest of the economy are especially interesting. In many countries which have developed as a result of a foreign-induced growth of exports, this has not given rise to more general development of the economy as a whole. Many of the richest countries today are testimony to the classical belief that development can be transmitted through trade but it remains true that in some of the underdeveloped countries a strong secular growth of exports has failed to carry over substantially to other sectors and has therefore not led to more widespread development in the domestic economy. As so often with popular beliefs, the degree of insulation within the enclave is often exaggerated, but the problem is real enough in many countries. Sometimes foreign investment which promoted the growth of an export sector is held responsible: its backwash effect is said to be the explanation for the failure of development to be propelled forward. But, to quote G. M. Meier,

There is little foundation to the assertion that if there had been no foreign investment a poor country would have generated more domestic investment; or that in the absence of foreign entrepreneurs, the supply of local entrepreneurs would have been larger (Meier, 1970, p. 510).

Contrary to the critics of foreign investment the real choice was not between employing resources in the export sector or in production for the local market, but rather between using surplus resources of land and labour to create an export industry or leaving them idle. But why did export growth before the war not have a greater effect in stimulating production for the local market? One way to find an answer is to notice that there have in fact been pronounced differences in the 'spread effect' of different sorts of exports. Even if one accepts as a starting point that induced development had nowhere gone very far, it is still instructive to notice that it had gone further in countries such as those of West Africa and Uganda where exports were produced by small cultivators than in those like Tanganyika or Northern Rhodesia where they were produced on plantations (sisal) or in mines (copper). The spread effect of any given export activity will depend on the nature of the export good in question. The main determinants are presumably, first, how the value added is distributed between domestic payments and payments to foreign-owned factors of production. In copper mining a relatively high proportion of value added accrues to overseas investors thus reducing correspondingly the amount of local purchasing power created. The second determinant of the 'spread effect' is the amount of forward and backward linkage that is likely to give rise to further local activities. Most primary product exports give rise to some forward linkage in the form of processing that must be done before export, either, as in the case of sisal and sugar, because extraction is technically only feasible immediately after harvesting, or, as in the case of copper, because transport costs are greatly reduced by smelting the metal from the rock before export. These then constitute forward linkage effects. Backward linkage is usually weak but if the modernization of agriculture leads to large increases in the use of, for example, artificial fertilizers or barbed wire, this might eventually bring about local production of these inputs, whilst mining is less likely to have backward linkage effects, and relies very largely on imports because of the specialized nature of its equipment (cf. Baldwin's (1966) excellent study, especially chapter 7).

Thirdly, the strength of the spread effect will depend on whether or not the export activity introduces new methods of production or new skills that can be applied to other sectors or activities in the economy. In this respect, grafting an export crop onto an existing farm sector will have spread effects in the measure in which it introduces new farm techniques that might also be applied to crops grown for consumption on the farm.

We have examined the ways in which international trade might lead to economic growth and have argued that the strength of the spread effect of trade will to some extent depend on the properties of the products being traded. We have also examined some theoretical objections to the conventional theory of international trade. The idea that international trade can benefit underdeveloped countries has also been attacked on empirical grounds, notably by Raoul Prebisch, the former Director General of UNCTAD and for many years Executive Secretary of UNECLA. Put briefly, Prebisch and others have argued that in the long run the terms of trade have a tendency to move against primary producers and that, since most underdeveloped countries are primary producers and exporters of primary products, it is in their long-term interest to industrialize and to use protective tariffs in the process (UNECLA, 1949; Prebisch, 1950).

The 'Prebisch Thesis' began with a study of the terms of trade of Great Britain, predominantly an exporter of manufactures and importer of primary products. Prebisch compared her terms of trade between 1876–80 and 1938 and found that they had improved from 163 to 100, and concluded from this that during this long period the terms of trade of the primary producing underdeveloped countries – he calls them the periphery countries – had seriously deteriorated in relation to Great Britain and other 'centre' countries. Moreover, he and others argue, this tendency is likely to continue because it is no more than a reflection of underlying economic trends. The main reason is that the fruits of technical progress accrue solely to the centre countries. When there is technical progress in manufacturing the periphery countries should in principle benefit from the ensuing fall in the prices of their imports, but prices do not fall because manufacturers operate under conditions of imperfect competition and are thus able to prevent prices from falling. Moreover, they do not face a perfect market in the factors they employ: the labour market is dominated by trade unions which are able to claim for their members part of the fruits of technical progress. So, the proceeds of improved methods of production are alleged to accrue in part to capitalists in the form of higher profits and in part to the trade unions in the form of higher wages. The consumer has no share in it and since the only way that the primary producing countries could benefit is through lower prices of their imports, their gain is zero.

If there is technical progress in the processes of production in the periphery countries the reverse happens. Unlike manufacturers, primary producers operate under competitive conditions both domestically and internationally. Consequently prices are reduced by technical progress and the benefits flow to the consumer, in this case the centre countries which import their food and raw materials.

Indeed Prebisch goes further than this and adduces figures to show that there is also a long-term disparity in the demand for manufactures and primary products. In the centre countries the income elasticity of demand for primary products is less than unity while in the peripheral countries that for manufactured goods exceeds one. Thus, in the USA the increase in the demand for imports of primary products is 0·66 of 1 per cent for every 1 per cent increase in **GDP** whilst in Latin America on average every 1 per cent increase in **GDP** is associated with a 1·58 per cent rise in the demand for (manufactured) imports. Why should this be so? First, because of the operation of Engel's Law: as incomes rise, so the proportion of them that is spent on food declines and consequently the demand for food increases less rapidly than the rise in incomes. Secondly, the demand for raw materials is checked by competition from synthetic, or man-made substances. The first time this happened was in in the 1920s when rayon – described universally as 'artificial silk' – began to compete in the market for both silk and cotton. Nylon and a whole range of fibres based on petro-chemicals followed – polyamides, polyesters and acrylic fibres including 'orlon' which constitutes a substitute for wool, the demand for which has also been affected by the increasing diffusion of central heating and heated vehicles which have led to lighter clothes than were formerly used in the countries that have cold winters.[2] The demand for rubber, first greatly enhanced by the phenomenal growth of the automobile industry then found itself faced with a rival in the form of synthetic rubber. Jute, hemp and sisal now compete with synthetic 'plastics' as packing materials and with nylon and other polyesters for making string, twine and ropes. Laminates compete with wood and, in all, there is very little for which a synthetic substitute does not exist. Where 'natural' raw materials continue to be employed, new techniques of production, e.g. in iron extraction and the manufacture of steel, economize in their use, and the growing preference for lightness in all things has reduced the metal content of machines and cars as well as the fibre content of clothes.

Having developed the Prebisch thesis at some length, let us now examine it critically. First, is it in fact true that the

2. The brilliant advertisement that appeared in the 1950s on the hoarding's of London's Underground:

In winter warm, in summer cool,
there is no substitute for wool!

is clearly no longer true. Today 38 per cent of world production of fibres are man-made (*The Times*, 3rd December 1970, p. 27).

improvement in Great Britain's terms of trade between the 1870s and 1938 was at the expense of underdeveloped countries? The answer depends critically in part on the way in which British trade statistics are customarily expressed, viz. that her exports are valued f.o.b. and her imports c.i.f.[3] It has to be remembered that during the period in question ocean freight rates fell dramatically, so that an improvement in Great Britain's terms of trade will have been in part the result of lower freight charges, not lower prices paid to the exporters.

Secondly, by no means all, or even the greater part, of Britain's imports came from the underdeveloped countries. In 1938 69 per cent of Britain's imports of primary products came from other countries of Europe, North America, Australia and New Zealand (Annual statement of the Trade of the United Kingdom, 1938, vol. 1, HMSO, 1939). This finding is related to a third criticism to which the Prebisch thesis lays itself open: a deterioration in the net barter terms of trade – and this is what was measured – does not necessarily make a county worse off if it occurs as a consequence of still greater improvements in productivity. If evidence is required, we have only to remember the fall of wheat prices in the course of the opening up of the American West during the latter part of the nineteenth century. It was the falling prices made possible by the opening up of highly productive virgin land which enabled American farmers to conquer the markets of Europe and to prosper in consequence. Similarly Gold Coast cacao farmers were able to create for themselves much higher incomes by entering the world market at a lower cost than their competitors. It is no accident that until recently the GDP per head of population of Ghana was more than twice that of any other tropical African country. The mistake is to confuse the static 'terms of trade' with the dynamic 'gains from trade'.

Finally there is always an intrinsic problem in comparing prices over long periods, because the goods sold at these prices

3. 'Free on board' meaning that carriage and insurance are *excluded* from the valuation; 'cost, insurance and freight' meaning that insurance and carriage from the port of embarkation are *included* in the valuation.

change. Whilst the primary products of the 1880s were probably not so very different from those sold sixty years later, the manufactured goods almost without exception had changed. A model 'T' Ford of 1908 was hardly to be compared with a car of 1938; machines were likely to be far more productive, soap more efficient. In addition the whole composition of exports had changed and included new products like cars and radios which were not yet produced in 1880.

We have seen that the Prebisch thesis is open to many kinds of objection. But it may of course still be true that although his case up to 1938 is not proven, the post-Second World War period – which is what really matters in the current context – shows Prebisch to have been quite right to warn underdeveloped countries against relying on primary product exports for their salvation. Here again however it is advisable to move cautiously. During and after the Second World War the terms of trade moved in favour of primary producers and this culminated in the boom following the outbreak of the Korean War in 1950. Since the mid-fifties the tide has however turned if one excludes oil and the net barter terms of trade for many commodities produced by low income countries have moved adversely, though the degree of adverse movement has varied greatly from commodity to commodity and from time to time. When attention is switched from the net barter terms of trade to the income terms of trade, which take account of changes in the *volume* of exports as well as the *prices* of exports and imports, it becomes clear that even in the years since the Korean boom the position of the primary produce exporting countries has improved, although less so than that of the developed countries (Wilson et al., 1969). But to say that their position has improved less is very different from the assertion that it has deteriorated and that primary producing countries have actually been impoverished.

As the Prebisch thesis has proved so vulnerable the grounds for advocating the development of manufacturing industries rather than primary products have shifted from a preoccupation with the terms of trade to a comparison of the total export proceeds of developed and low income countries. It is pointed out that whilst total world exports have increased vastly since the Second World War, the exports of primary products have increased much more slowly than the exports of manufactures and also the export increase of primary products from low income countries has been even smaller than the increase from developed countries. For instance during the years 1953–66 the increases of export proceeds *per decade* were as follows:

Table 1 Percentage increase per decade in world exports between 1953 and 1966 and shares of trade

	% *increase*	
Total trade	102 (104)[1]	
Primary products		
All countries	57 (50)	
Developed	70 (74)	
Underdeveloped	44 (20)	
Manufactured goods		
All countries	150	
Developed	152	
Underdeveloped	121	

Shares of underdeveloped countries exports in –	*1953*	*1966*
	%	%
Total exports	30	21
Primary exports	50	45
Manufactured exports	8	7

1. Figures in parentheses are for exports excluding fuel.
Source: based on Kravis (1970, Table 2, p. 862).

Table 1 shows that between 1953 and 1966 the decennial rate of growth of exports from the developed countries was 122 per cent whilst the rate of growth of primary product exports was only 57 per cent or if one takes those emanating from underdeveloped countries alone and ignores fuels, 20 per cent. Such comparisons can be very persuasive but they give little guidance to policy makers. First, they give no indication whether the slow rate of growth of exports of primary products from the low income countries is in fact the result of sluggish demand, as is usually taken for granted, or of factors holding back the expansion of supply. Kravis, in the very stimulating article from which this table is taken argues that supply factors may have been a very important part of the explanation. Thus the pessimism about the prospects for foreign exchange earnings from traditional exports often led to policies in the post Second World War period that directly or indirectly shifted incomes out of agriculture and into the public or industrial sector. These policies, he argues, included tariffs and other trade restrictions designed to encourage import substitution in the manufacturing sector, over-valued currencies and methods of taxation which redistributed income from the agricultural to the industrial and public sector (see chapter 6 below).

'The traditional export sectors', he continues, 'were not given normal incentives to expand and were saddled with high costs for their manufactured and imported inputs, and the entire agricultural sector with whatever potential it may have had for developing new exports in a world with more and more people to feed, was placed under similar handicaps' (Kravis, 1970, pp. 863–4).

The low rate of growth of primary product exports from low income countries cannot be solely attributed to unfavourable markets for commodities produced wholly or mainly in these countries since the export of these commodities – viz. coffee, tea, cocoa, bananas, tin and spices – only account for one quarter of their total exports, even when petrol is excluded. The other three quarters faces competition from substitutes or 'like' commodities produced in the developed countries. It is in these categories, particularly grains, fruits, vegetables, and oils and oil seeds, that the low income countries lost market opportunities (Cairncross, 1962, chs 12 and 13).

Quite distinct from the question of the long-term prospects for producers of food and raw materials is that of price instability in the short-run. It is often said that prices of primary products are peculiarly unstable. Demand for them is inelastic in the short-run and subject to shifts brought about by cyclical fluctuations in the buying countries. At the same time the short-run supply is said to be equally inelastic and equally subject to erratic shifts occasioned by the forces of nature: a drought or disease can decimate a crop; or the weather may produce a bumper harvest. Consequently prices are said to be very volatile. In general, price fluctuations in the post-war period have however been more often caused by changes in demand than by changes in supply. The reason is that very few crops are grown only, or even predominantly, in one country. It is improbable that crop disease or drought will affect all the countries growing a particular crop simultaneously and consequently, the effect of a sudden change in supply in one country will not greatly affect the world market price of the commodity in question. The instability of prices for primary products are compared with the prices of manufactured goods which fluctuate very little and which are said to be on a ratchet that prevents them from falling so that their movement is all in one direction. Underdeveloped countries which are dependent upon the export of primary products are thus said to face great fluctuations in their export proceeds whilst their import prices are at best constant but, more typically, rising. The point is sometimes made by saying that a recession in the industrial countries manifests itself in unemployment for factory workers at home and in falling prices for farmers in the primary producing countries.

These statements call for careful examination. First, how great have the price fluctuations in fact been? There is no doubt that before the War they were at times very great. For instance a League of Nations report of 1943 states:

During the last twenty years the price of wheat and jute has been halved three times within about twelve months; the price of cotton three times in periods of under eighteen months, the price of copper and lead was halved four times within periods of two years and doubled three times even more rapidly (quoted by Caine, 1966, p. 12).

But even that does not tell us a great deal for what matters is not only the extremes of price fluctuation but also how much

was sold at these extreme prices. If three quarters of a crop
is sold at a median price, the fact that the remaining quarter
was sold at very different prices has a different significance
than if three quarters of the crop was sold at the two extreme
ends of the price spectrum.

But whilst price fluctuations have continued since the War
the degree of amplitude appears to have been much smaller.
Indeed, Professor A. MacBean, who is one of the first to have
subjected received dogma about short-term fluctuations to the
test of careful empirical analysis, has cast great doubt on
many of the ideas that one had hitherto taken for granted
(MacBean, 1966, ch. 2). Rather than look at price fluctuations, MacBean defines export instability as short-term
fluctuations in export *earnings* which is the more relevant
concept. His findings which relate to the period 1946–58 are
as follows:

1. Underdeveloped countries do indeed have less stable export
earnings than the average developed country, but the difference is
not large and there is a considerable overlap in experience between
rich and poor countries. (p. 36)

2. Although some developed countries are predominantly exporters
of primary products they are untypical whilst it would be true to
say that the typical underdeveloped country is heavily specialized in
primary product exports. (p. 37)

3. It is true that fluctuations in the export earnings of the average
primary producing country have been greater than for the average
industrial country, but the latter's export earnings are not as stable
as is commonly supposed and consequently the difference in their
fluctuations of export earnings is not so great either.

4. But the experience of instability revealed by different commodities is extremely diverse. The important distinction is not between
goods which are produced in factories and goods which are grown
on the land or extracted from the earth. The crucial distinctions lie
in the variability of demand and supply and in the short-run re-
sponses of demand and supply to changes in price. These factors
vary much more among primary products and among manufactures
than they do between the two classes of goods. (pp. 39–40)

5. Export instability in underdeveloped countries seems to stem

more from quantity fluctuations than from changes in price. This suggests that policies which aim solely at price stabilization may remove relatively little of the export instability and in some cases may even increase fluctuations in total proceeds. (pp. 56–7)

Smaller swings in export earnings are, of course, in large part the consequence of smaller swings in economic activity in the more industrially developed countries. In Great Britain, for example, where during the inter-war years unemployment never fell below 10 per cent, it has never since risen to 4 per cent.

They may also in part have been the result of international and national measures to reduce these fluctuations. A number of international commodity agreements have been in operation for varying periods since the War, among them the international coffee and sugar agreements. These usually take the form of a guaranteed price for a given quantity which is allocated to the various producer countries by quotas. The basic objective of these agreements has usually been simply to *stabilize* prices by providing a guaranteed market for a restricted volume of output and this could be said to be in the interest of both producing and consuming countries. Some agreements have however, gone further and sought to 'support' rather than just stabilize prices, i.e. to raise them above the level that would obtain in the absence of the agreement.

Even the simple 'stabilizing' agreements have usually proved difficult to maintain because there is a basic conflict of interest between producer and consumer countries. The former naturally seek the highest possible price for their crops, but if they are successful in raising it above the free market equilibrium there will be a temptation to increase supply beyond the amounts agreed. Governments that are signatories to the agreement may be able to prevent their own farmers from falling prey to the temptation, but the higher price will also cause countries that had not hitherto grown the crop, and which were therefore not signatories to the agreement to start growing it in the hope of being able to sell at slightly below the guaranteed price but still above the previously prevailing free market price. This will make the farmers in the signatory countries the more resentful at being restricted to a quota. At the same time, the consuming countries are tempted to buy at lower prices from countries not covered by the agreement. Not unnaturally, such agreements have therefore often broken down.

There is also a conflict of interest between producing countries themselves. High cost producers will want to go for a price which yields them a profit whilst low cost producers would sooner adopt a lower price in the hope that by cutting out the high cost producer, they will have a larger market. Given these conflicts of interest it is not surprising that since the War only five international commodity agreements have been successfully negotiated, viz. the agreements covering wheat, sugar, olive oil, tin and coffee. The wheat agreement hardly affects underdeveloped countries, the sugar agreement became inoperative when America suspended imports from Cuba; the olive oil agreement is limited to ensuring 'fair' competition and encouraging the growth of the market; the tin agreement alone has been really successful over a long period mainly because of a secular growth of demand; the coffee agreement, too, has been maintained successfully in the face of repeated near-breakdowns (Killick, 1967).

National measures of stabilization have mostly taken the form of setting up marketing boards and the imposition of export taxes or both.

A marketing board is given the exclusive right to buy a crop from small farmers and to sell it directly, or by auction, to overseas buyers. It has been the common practice for marketing boards in Ghana, Nigeria and Uganda to fix a price to be paid to the farmers for a year ahead, in the hope that the removal of uncertainty would encourage farmers to expand production. Originally they went further and attempted to stabilize prices not only for one year but also over longer periods. This was done by establishing price stabilization funds which syphoned off part of the proceeds from export sales in good years and then used them to subsidize the price paid to growers in bad years.

In the early post-war years when the marketing boards were established, the general trend of commodity prices was secularly upwards and whilst producer prices were gradually raised it was always with a lag so that the stabilization funds grew ever larger. Arguably farmers might have produced more if producer prices had reflected world market prices more quickly and this could have yielded them higher incomes. One effect might have been a still greater boost to aggregate demand which might have led to faster growth of production of the things on which farmers wanted to spend their incomes. Subsequently, from the mid-50s onwards, commodity prices began to fall and the existence of the stabilization funds helped to cushion farmers from sudden falls in price.

One major weakness of trying to stabilize prices in this way is that marketing boards have found it impossible in practice to distinguish short-term fluctuations in price from long-term trends. Whilst short-term fluctuations may be a hindrance to economic progress because they are disruptive and discourage farmers from taking risks, long-term price trends should act as signals to indicate the desirability of increasing or curtailing output of a given crop. The marketing board structure may therefore have acted to reduce flexibility in switching from one crop to another. Marketing boards have also tended to be conservative; in the 1940s and early 1950s, as we have seen, they consistently underestimated the prospective world market price and ever since then they have often been unnecessarily concerned with their own solvency and have thus done less than they might have done to cushion farmers against falling prices. But the very concept of price stabilization is questionable because it implies that what farmers care most about is stable prices when it may well be that the aim ought to be to stabilize *incomes* rather than *prices*. Price stabilization may actually destabilize incomes if there are unforeseen increases or falls in output, since farmers' incomes are of course compounded of the size of their crop and the price they receive per unit of output. Some would go further and argue that any attempt to stabilize prices or incomes has a long-term cost in that it removes the need for business acumen from the great majority of the population who derive their livelihood from farming. Since economic progress depends in part on people with business acumen who are adept at responding to market signals, anything which denies people experience of operating in a free market will retard economic development. This thesis, whilst intrinsically plausible, is in practice virtually impossible to refute or substantiate with more than illustrative evidence. Some would therefore exclude such statements from books purporting to be concerned in general with 'positive' economics, but that would be excessively restrictive. The fact that a statement is difficult to substantiate or refute does not make it *ipso facto* less important or worthwhile to an understanding of economic processes.

What is, however, susceptible to empirical verification is the earlier statement that 'short-term fluctuations may be a hindrance to economic progress'. We are again indebted to Professor MacBean's painstaking statistical work, and his conclusions cast great doubt on the statement (MacBean, 1966, ch. 3; also reprinted in Livingstone, 1971, ch. 10). One often hears it said that fluctuations in export earnings cause corresponding fluctuations in the national incomes of the exporting countries because exports play such a prominent role in the economies of these countries. MacBean shows that not only is it not true that foreign trade is quantitatively more important for poor than for rich nations, but further, that 'there is no evidence of association between the magnitude of fluctuations in income and of fluctuations in exports. Countries with relatively stable incomes have had very unstable exports and vice versa' (p. 62).

It is also commonly thought that fluctuations in export earnings are an important factor in generating instability in domestic capital formation. Yet in some twenty underdeveloped countries investigated, MacBean could find no clear association between the magnitude of fluctuations in investment and in the importing power of exports. 'At most 12 per cent of the variation among countries in instability of investment seems attributable to the degree of instability of the importing power of their exports' (pp. 70–71).

In some countries the insensitivity of investment to fluctuations in exports may be partly explained by successful Government stabilization policy. For instance, progressive export taxes which rise and fall more than in proportion to changes in export prices have been widely used, and as we saw earlier, the operation of marketing boards should have moderated swings in producer incomes and so, in turn, dampened the variability of capital formation. But we also know that sometimes they had in fact the reverse effect (see MacBean, 1966, chs 5 and 10). Above all else it is important to remember that many underdeveloped countries enjoy in fact relatively stable export proceeds and that in several large countries containing the greater part of the world's population, including India, Pakistan, Brazil, Indonesia and mainland China, foreign trade is a relatively small proportion of GNP.

4 Models of Development

The simplest way to view economic development is to see it as an outward shift of a country's production possibility boundary. If the process is continuous, then each year the boundary shifts further outwards indicating that in the ensuing year the country can have more of both the 'goods' measured along the two axes, as the following diagram shows:

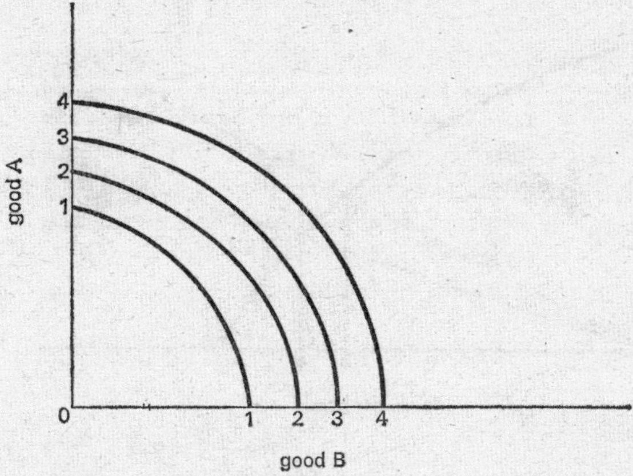

Figure 1

The diagram represents a country producing only two goods, A and B. The four boundaries correspond to the amounts of A and B that a country is able to produce in successive years. A country does not necessarily produce all it can, in which case it will be operating at some point below its current production possibility boundary, but what it cannot do is to produce more of A and B than the maxima indicated by the boundary. The diagram cannot tell us what combination of *A* and *B* will or should be produced because that must depend upon the relative valuations placed on *A* and *B*.

The diagram assumes that in any given year the country has a given quantum of resources or inputs and the production possibility boundary shows how much of *A* and *B* can be produced with various combinations of these inputs. If the boundary shifts outwards over time it must be either because there has been technical progress or because there have been increases in the available resources to use as inputs.

We are accustomed to thinking that such increases in inputs are the result of capital formation, and that there is a direct

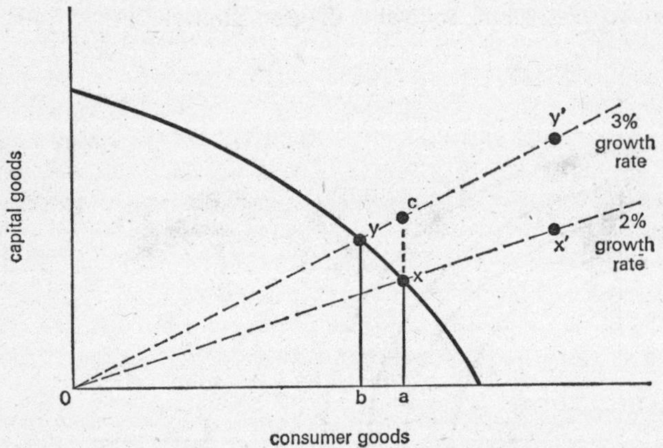

Figure 2

relationship between production possibilities in a given year and the amount of capital formation that has taken place in some earlier year. Since capital formation or the production of capital goods requires resources or inputs in just the same way as the production of other goods it follows that the more capital goods are produced in a given year the less other goods can be produced. There is therefore in this model an implied choice between present output and future output: the less a country produces for current consumption, the more of its resources can be devoted to capital formation. But capital formation enhances future productive capacity and consequently the possibility of future consumption. Countries, therefore, appear to have to choose between present and future consumption. The more a country is prepared to forego consumption at the present time, the greater will be its increment of productive resources and therefore of future consumption. These notions can be illustrated with a similar diagram in which we show the choice to be between the production of capital goods (y axis) and consumer goods (x axis)

Let us assume that the country is initially producing at point x where the rate of annual consumption is Oa and productive capacity is growing at 2 per cent per annum so that each year the production possibility boundary moves outwards by 2 per cent. If the economy continues to devote the same proportion of its resources to the production of capital goods, its path of growth will be along the ray labelled '2 per cent growth rate'. In twenty years the economy will reach the point x'.[1]

But supposing it came about that the rate of consumption was reduced by the amount ab and that capital formation (or, strictly speaking, the production of capital goods) went up correspondingly, then production would be shifted to point y. Since more capital goods are being produced, the growth rate will be increased. In this example it rises to 3 per cent and in twenty years the economy will be at point y'. The more rapid rate of growth is purchased at the expense of a lower rate of current consumption.

How does one decide whether it is worth it? Suppose that at point x 15 per cent of the country's resources were being devoted to capital goods production and the remaining 85 per cent were used to make consumer goods. Suppose then that the shift to point y meant a reallocation of resources so that 23 per cent were now being used to make capital goods. How long will it take to regain the loss in consumption if the

1. The exposition here follows almost verbatim that in Lipsey (1966, ch. 56). My excuse for this plagiarism is that I could think of no more lucid way of putting it!

shift to point y is made? It depends on what is meant by 'regaining the loss'. On the assumed figures it takes only three and one third years to reach point c where consumption is again Oa. Thus the actual reduction in living standards lasts only three and one third years. Of course, had the reallocation of resources not occurred, income would have expanded along the 2 per cent growth path and, thus, although the actual cut is restored in less than four years, consumption is still well below what it would have been if the reallocation in favour of capital formation had not taken place. In fact it takes ten years for the actual level of consumption to catch up to what it would have been had no reallocation occurred. As a matter of fact it takes an additional nine years after that before total consumption over the whole period is as large as it would have been if the economy had remained on the 2 per cent growth path. From year nineteen on the initial sacrifice yields bigger and bigger returns.

The figures in this example are, of course, hypothetical and intended only to illustrate the relationships under discussion. Much will depend on the rate of return. But even if a nineteen year waiting period before a fairly small shift of resources towards capital formation has paid off overstates the length of the waiting period, the example illustrates clearly some of the costs involved in achieving faster growth through reallocation of resources and suggests approximate orders of magnitude.

In advanced industrial countries it is clear that economic growth is by no means solely a function of the 'capital formation quotient'. New knowledge and inventions contribute markedly to the growth of national income and even the mere replacement of worn out machines by new ones that embody inventions which make them more productive will raise national income without any increase in the capital stock. Similarly, a healthier and more educated labour force contributes to economic growth. Both education and measures to improve health can be viewed as forms of capital formation and differ from the more conventional forms, like the building of power-stations, roads and factories, only in that they provide consumption goods and services simultaneously. Education, for example, is an end in itself, as well as a means to faster economic growth.

If it is the case in developed countries that the growth of output is only weakly associated with investment in physical capital, this is likely to be even more the case in underdeveloped countries. Economic development involves a change in the very structure of the economy and some argue that it involves major changes in social structure and in 'ideas and beliefs'. It is, however, becoming clear that economic development can occur under very diverse social, political and value systems and that the Western European or North American model with its emphasis on individualism, the nuclear family, and freedom to move, to hire and fire, etc., is not a necessary condition of development, as witness the experience of Japan, the Soviet Union and China.

The important question for the moment is whether a restriction of consumption as a matter of policy is in fact necessary or sufficient to promote economic development in underdeveloped countries in which, by definition, consumption is minimal to start with. The idea of the trade-off between current and future consumption has been very powerful in influencing development policy. It lay at the very heart of the Soviet Union's policy of forced industrialization in the 1920s and later, and has played a vital role in Communist China and in other countries that seek to model themselves on either of those two countries. But it also is a very influential notion amongst economists and others in a great many under-developed countries which are persuaded of the usefulness of economic planning without being socialist or communist. Sir W. Arthur Lewis has said that the 'central problem in the theory of economic development is to understand the process by which a community which was previously saving and investing 4 or 5 per cent of its national income or less, converts itself into an economy where voluntary saving is running at 12 to 15 per cent of national income or more' (Lewis, 1954), and this dictum is widely echoed in underdeveloped countries and in the national and international agencies concerned with providing aid. Admittedly those who point to the need for increased saving and capital formation more often advocate policies which peg consumption, rather than actually reduce it, so that policy is addressed to the ways in which one might maximize the reinvestment of increments to output and thus raise the capital formation quotient rather than how to reallocate existing resources in favour of capital formation. But the ideas in either case rest solidly on the analytical framework developed above.

How relevant is this framework. First, let us re-examine the assumptions. It will be recalled that a choice between consumption and capital formation has only to be made if the economy is in fact operating on its production possibility boundary, i.e. if all its productive resources are fully employed in the production of either one or the other. One could legitimately argue that this is the case in advanced industrial countries at times of full employment. But in underdeveloped countries it is frequently argued that the situation is typically different and that whilst it may often be the case that the capital stock is fully employed, this is not the case with the labour force. The literature on underdeveloped countries is peppered with references to surplus labour, underemployment and disguised unemployment.

Years ago it was fashionable to infer from the alleged existence of unemployment in low income countries that the way to promote development was to apply the policy tools created by J. M. Keynes and to institute measures such as deficit financing and public works programmes. This was soon seen to be unworkable because it was recognized that there is a crucial difference between 'Keynesian' unemployment in which not only labour but also machines and other productive resources were unused, owing to a lack of effective demand, and the unemployment observed in low income countries which was attributable rather to a lack of cooperant resources (cf. Bauer and Yamey, 1957, p. 75).

This latter type of unemployment of unskilled labour, reflecting a lack of cooperant resources of land or capital or skilled labour was a phenomenon with which the classical economists of the early nineteenth century were much concerned, and that is why it is often referred to as 'classical unemployment'. To combat classical unemployment with Keynesian measures is to provoke inflation or, alternatively, a balance of payments deficit if the increased spending of the newly employed is not matched by a domestic increase of 'wage goods' or consumer goods.

The existence of 'classical unemployment' has caused a number of economists to develop models of development derived from classical economic theory rather than from the type of 'choice' analysis that was portrayed at the beginning of this chapter and which is often called 'neo-classical'. Models derived from the classical tradition are not so much concerned with the reallocation of resources as with the harnessing of unemployed resources.

The best known of these models of development is that of Lewis (1954). Lewis postulates the existence of a subsistence sector with surplus labour and he sees in this the seed for the development of a capitalist sector which draws its labour from the subsistence sector. The distinguishing characteristic of the capitalist sector is that it uses reproducible capital and that it produces for profit. This sector need not necessarily make manufactured goods but could also include mines and plantations. Nor need it necessarily be private, but could equally well be a public sector provided only that, e.g. like British nationalized industries, it hires labour to produce an output which is to be sold for profit. In the subsistence sector output per head is much lower and the marginal product of some labourers may be zero, or, at least, less than the average product so that there is disguised unemployment or underemployment. The capitalist sector then draws its labour from the subsistence sector and it is assumed that as a result of rapid increases in population (especially in countries that are densely populated to start with) the supply of unskilled labour is unlimited. Although most of the labour will come from subsistence agriculture others will come from over-manned occupations such as domestic service, petty trade and casual work. Their supply is said to be 'unlimited' in the sense that capitalists can obtain ever increasing supplies of such labour at the existing wage rate, i.e. they will not have to raise wages to attract more labour. The capitalist sector can therefore expand indefinitely at a constant wage rate for unskilled labour. The actual wage rate will be determined by earnings in the subsistence sector, but 'earnings' in this case means the average product and not the marginal product, because conventionally every one in the subsistence sector receives an equal share of what is produced. Capitalists will have to pay some margin – perhaps 30 per cent – above average subsistence pay because the surplus workers need some incentive to move and in any case part of the difference is needed to compensate them for the higher urban cost of living.

In the subsistence sector labour is employed up to the point where its marginal product is zero but in the capitalist sector labour will only be employed up to the point where its marginal product equals the wage since a capitalist employer would be reducing his surplus if he paid labour more than he receives for what is produced.

This surplus is the key to the process of development as displayed in Lewis's model, as appears in the diagram on the following page.

OS is the amount a man would receive in the subsistence sector, i.e. the average product of that sector. OW is the capitalist wage. With a given initial quantum of capital, the demand for labour is initially represented by the marginal productivity schedule of labour NQ. If we assume profit maximization, labour will then be applied up to the point where the wage W, equals marginal productivity, i.e. Q, corresponding to Oa workers. Workers in excess of Oa will earn whatever they can in the subsistence sector.

Development takes place because part of what is produced accrues to the capitalist in the form of a surplus, shown in the diagram by the area WN_1Q_1, and this is reinvested. The reinvestment produces an increase in the amount of fixed capital and this is seen in the diagram to cause a shift in the marginal product of labour curve from N_1Q_1 to N_2Q_2 in the next period. More labour will now be employed and the surplus increases, leading to a further shift of the curve to N_3Q_3

where yet more labour is drawn in from the subsistence sector and the surplus is greater still. The process will continue until all surplus labour in the subsistence sector has been drawn into the capitalist sector. When that happens pay in the subsistence sector will start to rise, causing wages in the capitalist sector to rise, and then the first phase of development will have ceased as the supply curve of labour has ceased to be horizontal, but has turned upwards.

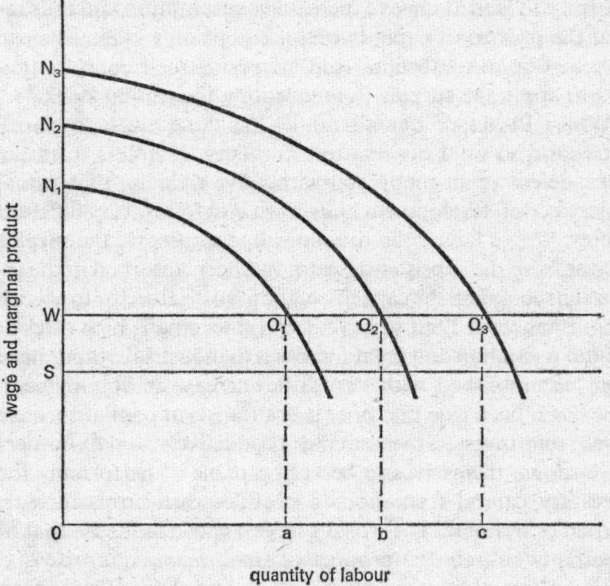

Figure 3

Before leaving the exposition of the 'Lewis model' we should draw attention to two more features of it. First, it should be noted that Lewis is certain that only capitalists – be they private or the state – can be relied upon to both save and to reinvest the surplus into productive capital assets. Neither peasants, wage earners, landlords, nor the professional classes will engage in capital formation. They may save in order to educate their children or for old age but 'there is really only one class that is pretty certain to reinvest its profits, productively, and that is the class of industrialists'.

Secondly, following on from what was just said, the 'Lewis model' is not primarily concerned with the question of how to increase the supply of consumer goods in the short run. On the contrary its essential feature is the reinvestment of an ever larger surplus in order to enlarge a country's capital stock. Higher wages, rents, professional earnings or earnings in agriculture will lead at once to increased consumption and thus retard the process of capital accumulation: only capitalists can be relied upon to abstain from increasing their consumption and to apply the surplus to augmenting the capital stock.[2]

Whilst Professor Lewis's model has done much to clarify issues and to weld observation to theory, it suffers from the same defect as so many comprehensive models; that actual experience of development has shown it to follow very different routes. Wages have risen dramatically long before the surplus labour from the subsistence sector has been absorbed in the industrial sector and the capacity of the industrial sector to absorb labour has turned out to have been rather small: high rates of capital formation and great increases in industrial output have been accomplished with very little increase in employment. Nor has it been true that only industrialists or capitalists have saved, and invested their savings productively. Small farmers have shown themselves to be very capable of performing the necessary capital formation to produce cash crops for sale abroad or at home. The world's largest cocoa industry, that of Ghana, is entirely the product of small farm enterprise and capital formation, as Bauer (1957) and Hill (1963) have reminded us. More recently small farmers in Pakistan have been largely responsible for the large-scale installation of irrigation tubewells that have helped to revolutionize the

2. This brief summary does scant justice to one of the most stimulating and revealing articles in the literature on economic development. The model is developed in a more rigorous form which claims to remove some of the ambiguities and technical short-comings, by Professors Ranis and Fei (1961, 1964).

yields of rice and wheat. Lewis to some extent covers himself against this criticism by treating such farmers as part of the capitalist sector and not the subsistence sector; but whilst that may leave his model formally intact, its failure to explain the actual experience of development in some low income countries must make it seem irrelevant even if it does not actually refute it.

This type of model is open to other criticisms. Although, for example, Lewis's theory is supposed to explain development in market economies it singularly fails to do so since it contains no immediate answer to the question 'who will buy what is produced?' In a market economy even the extreme types of capital goods ('machines to make machines') need buyers if 'capitalists' are to produce them. Since the theory is intended to demonstrate how to maximize capital accumulation by minimizing any consequent increase in consumption it is difficult to understand what purpose any businessman may have in producing capital or consumer goods for which no demand is generated. It assumes automatic reinvestment in an economy in which businessmen cannot have any conceivable motive to reinvest. It may therefore prove to be restricted in relevance to economies in which all production is in the hands of the state.

Another criticism to level against this type of model is that it assumes the existence of entrepreneurs who will act in the way specified. This simply assumes away one of the major problems of economic development which is to recognize and to create the conditions in which entrepreneurs come into being. Again, if the model is restricted to State dominated countries this need not be a problem though it is still open to question as to whether the absence of an entrepreneurial class *ipso facto* endows the public sector with an ample supply of the appropriate talents! (Hirschman, 1958, p. 54).

We have yet to examine whether disguised unemployment or underemployment is in fact widespread in the densely populated countries of India, Egypt and Jamaica which Lewis had principally in mind. This is critically important for 'classical' type theories of development because they assume that a considerable amount of surplus rural labour can be removed without reducing total agricultural output. Since there will then be more food left for those remaining on the land, this can be extracted for the use of those who have been removed to work in the 'modern' sector, without reducing *per capita* consumption. Many of the earlier studies of the 1930s and 1940s estimated the volume of surplus labour by deducting the quantity of labour required for the production of the current level of output, from the adult agrarian population. But one major weakness of this method was that it did not allow for the seasonal nature of agricultural work. The critical test is whether the agricultural labour force is fully employed during peak periods of demand for labour, such as planting and harvesting. Only if labour is redundant during peak periods of demand could the agricultural labour force be reduced without reducing agricultural output. In a review of recent empirical studies Professor D. W. Jorgenson concludes that

when account is taken of the seasonality of demands for agricultural labor, the situation in south-eastern Europe, Egypt, China and south-east Asia appears to be one of labor shortage rather than labor surplus (Jorgensen, 1967, reprinted in Livingstone, 1971, p. 70).

Attempts have also been made to test the existence of disguised unemployment directly, by observing what has happened to agricultural output when substantial parts of the agricultural labour force have been withdrawn in a short period of time – either for a public works project, or as a result of famine or epidemic. Examining a large number of such cases and also studies by social anthropologists, Professor T. W. Schultz concludes that the idea of zero marginal productivity of labour in agriculture is a myth. 'There is no evidence of any poor country anywhere', he writes, 'that would even suggest that a transfer of a small fraction, say 5 per cent, of the existing labour force in agriculture with other things equal, could be made without reducing its production' (Schultz, 1956). It is now generally accepted that disguised unemployment in excess of – say – 5 per cent is very rare in under-developed countries.

One must not misunderstand however, what is being refuted. None of the studies investigated the possibility of maintaining agricultural output in the face of a falling labour force by a change in the organization or techniques of farming. Those, like Nurkse (1953) and Rosenstein-Rodan (1943) who had asserted the existence of surplus labour may have had it in mind that there might need to be changes in farm organization or method before the surplus labour could be released. But as soon as such changes are stipulated the idea of surplus labour freely available for work in a new sector of the economy must be abandoned because the necessary changes in agriculture cannot be accomplished without a cost in resources or 'investment' broadly conceived.

Much will depend, of course, on whether the cost is large or small. In many countries it may well be that very small changes in technique would enable output to be maintained when the numbers on the farm are reduced. Whilst these changes will have *some* cost it may be very small. Secondly, no one denies the seasonality in the demand for labour in agriculture, so that whilst it may well be that labour cannot be spared at peak seasons there is considerable disguised unemployment at other times. If that is the case, the 'surplus' labour might not be very useful as a supply to urban industry where continuous opera-tion may be essential, but it could be utilized for rural public works that could be suspended during the peak agricultural season. Indeed one should not even conclude too readily that an annual scheduled closure of a factory is necessarily impos-sible. Many plants in the advanced industrial countries close down during the peak holiday season in July or August and require their workers to take their holidays then.

In much of the writing which is premised on surplus or redundant labour in agriculture, there is also a confusion between the marginal product of labour and the product of the marginal labourer. Myint explains admirably what is at issue by an example (Myint, 1967, pp. 86–7). Suppose that when thirty hours of work is put into a family holding the marginal product of the thirtieth hour falls to zero. There is nothing irrational about applying labour to land until the marginal product of the 30th hour of work falls to zero; since labour is free it would be wasteful not to squeeze the most out of the scarce factor which is land. Now suppose that there are six workers in the family who share the work equally, so that each has to work five hours a day. With given agricultural techniques the total output of the farm will only remain unchanged as successive workers are removed, provided those who stay behind are willing to work longer to make up the total of thirty hours a day. It should however be noted that this would involve harder or longer hours of work for those who remain on the land. Generally, they will only do this if they are offered some incentive. It is arguable that a five hour day constitutes disguised unemployment, or that the pace of work is such as to leave time to watch the birds whilst working (Sen, 1968, p. 5). But clearly those who remain behind will not work longer or harder if they can continue to obtain the same amount of food as hitherto by working only five hours. If total output is not to decline they must be offered an economic incentive to work longer or more intensively. If a system of forced deliveries, as in Russia in the 1920s, is ruled out, then farmers will produce the surplus food only if in exchange they are offered manufactured goods produced by those who have left agriculture. In that case, however, we are no longer in a situation where the social cost of using disguised unemployment is zero. The social cost of not letting agricultural output fall is made up of the resources used to manufacture the incentive consumer goods which are needed to induce those who remain on the land to work harder or longer or to adopt new techniques of production. In the short-run it may be possible, of course, to levy taxes on farmers which will ensure that production is kept up if the consumption of those who remain on the land is not to fall. But such forcible methods seldom work except as temporary expedients. In the long-run, the modernization of the economy, including agriculture, is more likely to take place in response to positive incentives than by coercion. The need for positive incentives is especially great in countries where there is hunger and where a removal of people from the farm might lead ,not to a fall in output, but to an increase in consumption by those who remain behind. There then occurs an increase in the total demand for food, while supply remains unchanged and this manifests itself in a shortage of food in the towns; food has to be imported and paid for with scarce foreign exchange. The creation of employment opportunities to absorb the 'disguised unemployed' can be justified only if their output is more than enough to cover the extra consumption which is generated. If the 'disguised unemployed' are used to build roads and other public utilities rather than in directly productive activities there will be no immediate increase in consumer goods.

Post-Keynesian growth models

Whilst a 'classical' type of model of economic development has dominated academic discussion of the subject, those concerned with development policy have more often had resort to macroeconomic theories of the post-Keynesian type. It will be remembered that Keynes's theory of income determination was essentially confined to the explanation of short-term variations in income and output. Investment plays a critical role in short-term income determination, because if there is less than full employment an increase in investment will lead to an increase in employment and income. But Keynes was not primarily concerned with the long run effects of investment on output, once the new machines and other capital goods came into production. Yet it is these long-term effects of capital formation that are the principal concern of governments in low income countries.

Extensions of Keynes's theory into the long-run led to the formulation of a concept called the incremental capital–output ratio. This ratio expresses the amount of net capital formation associated with a given increase in output. Thus if it takes three pounds in net capital formation to achieve an increase in annual output of one pound, then the incremental capital–output ratio (ICOR) is said to be three. Such a ratio can in principle be calculated for a particular project or for an industry or for the economy as a whole. In the latter case the ICOR expresses the amount of capital required to attain a given increase in national output or income. From here it is an easy step to calculate what proportion of national income needs to be saved (and invested) to achieve given increases in GNP. If a country aims to raise GNP by 5 per cent a year, and the incremental capital–output ratio is assumed to be three, then it will have to save and invest 3×5 per cent $= 15$ per cent of its GNP. Suppose, however, that population is increasing by 2 per cent a year and that the aim is really to increase income *per head* by 5 per cent, then GNP must rise by 2 per cent per annum just to keep income per head from falling, so that the total increase of GNP will need to be about 7 per cent a year and given the same ICOR of three, this implies that the country would need to save and devote to capital formation 21 per cent of its national income. This makes no allowance for the need to make good the depreciation of the existing capital stock and the figure of 21 per cent is therefore for *net* capital formation.

Many Development Plans of low income countries will be found to contain calculations of 'savings requirements' based on these relationships. Development Plans usually take the form of planned increases in GNP for a period of years ahead, and a model which purports to predict the amount of capital formation required to achieve given target rates of growth of GNP is naturally very attractive.

Sometimes these relationships are also used to calculate the amount of foreign aid 'required' to attain the target rates of growth. If it is manifestly impossible to achieve a rate of savings of 21 per cent out of domestic income, then, it is argued, the difference between the amount that can be saved and the amount of capital 'required' must be provided in the form of foreign investment or foreign aid.

The idea of an overall incremental capital–output ratio was originally formulated in the late 1930s and 1940s in the post-Keynesian analysis of mature economies. This analysis attempted to find an answer to the question of how much national income had to grow in order to induce sufficient investment to maintain that rate of growth. It was feared that income might not grow fast enough to provide a market for the increased output resulting from investment in earlier periods. But the problem of low income countries is not how to sustain a certain rate of growth but rather how to bring about changes in the economy which will make growth possible. It is a problem of 'transformation' rather than of 'growth'. One should not expect a theory of 'growth' to be a theory of development, since this would require an explanation of the process by which a backward economy is structurally transformed.

The overall incremental capital–output ratio has in any case proved much less stable than was at first supposed, even in the advanced industrial countries for which it was originally formulated. It is of even more doubtful value for planning in the low income countries. First, it must be immediately obvious that the capital cost of a given increase in output must vary greatly from industry to industry and between directly productive activities and social overhead capital projects. Clearly, it is likely to be much higher in public utilities than in manufacturing. Secondly, the capital–output ratio is greatly affected by the choice of technique and by the efficiency with which capital formation is undertaken. One can to some extent allow for differences in the capital–output ratio of different types of project by deriving the overall ratio from weighted ratios for each proposed investment activity, but in practice, attempts to anticipate ICORs on an industry basis have usually been subject to wide margins of error. Finally, it is not sensible to imagine that the rate of economic development of a low income or any other country can be mechanically related to inputs of capital alone. The national income will also be affected by the growth of entrepreneurship, and by changes in attitude and institutions which favour the growth of output. The conventional way of measuring capital formation can also leave out of account inputs that may have a significant effect on productivity. For instance, expenditure on education – or investment in human capital, as it has come to be called – is unlikely to be included in a conventional computation of capital formation, and yet it may be critically important in determining indirectly the size of the conventional capital–

output ratio. Studies in advanced countries have shown that only a part of growth during the past few decades can be explained by reference to increases in capital or labour, and that a large part must be attributed to a 'residual factor' in which the growth of knowledge and skill, disseminated by education, is thought to play an important role.

If the capital–output ratio has proved a poor analytical device in mature economies, the relationship between capital and output is likely to be still more tenuous, unstable and unpredictable in underdeveloped countries. The overall ratio for the economy as a whole is particularly vulnerable in countries in which a large proportion of income is derived from farming, as a good or bad harvest can greatly affect national output and income and is quite independent of capital investment. Moreover, agricultural output may be greatly affected by small investment projects undertaken by the farmers themselves. Official statistics of capital formation generally ignore these, as we saw in chapter 1. Also, new farm techniques which require little capital formation as conventionally measured, have brought about substantial increases in output. Given these difficulties of measurement, an overall ICOR calculated from the past relationship between aggregate capital formation and national income may therefore grossly underestimate the amount of income likely to be associated with a given capital expenditure programme.

An exclusive preoccupation with capital–output ratios also tends to deflect attention from ways of raising output that do not require investment. For example, existing plant may not be fully utilized or it may be possible to increase output of manufactures by going over to shift work instead of an eight-hour day, especially if there is urban unemployment, as is so often the case.

In conclusion, simple macroeconomic planning models of the kind that have been discussed here tend to lay undue stress on the need to save in order to accumulate capital. Whilst it is generally the case that periods of rapid growth of income have been associated with high rates of capital formation there can be no presumption that the former has been caused by the latter. One can equally argue that rapid growth of income encourages capital formation. To the extent that an economy relies on market forces for development, personal saving is as likely to retard development as it is to promote it. Saving is *not spending* and therefore reduces aggregate demand. It is only if the consequent slack in productive capacity can be transformed into productive capital formation that it may promote development. Both private businesses and Governments may in principle engage in productive capital formation, including investment in human capital. But official exhortations to save so that governments can use the proceeds to build monumental blocks of offices probably do nothing to promote a rise in the standard of life.

The models considered in this chapter are highly aggregative; they all view the economy as if it had only two scarce factors and as if it were producing only a single product. Consequently they throw no light on such vitally important questions as 'what should be produced' and 'what techniques of production should one use'? Yet these questions require an answer because whilst there may well be several *feasible* development paths or strategies, there may only be one that is *optimal*. This issue is taken up in the next chapter in which development strategy is discussed against a background of less aggregative models.

5 Development Strategies

We saw in chapter 2 that one common explanation of under-development is that low income countries are held back by a chain of interlocking vicious circles. To many it has seemed that the only way of escape is to initiate a concerted programme of industrialization. To succeed, so it is said, this needs to be a carefully timed, massive drive along several fronts at once, so that each new industry benefits from the simultaneous development of other – complementary – industries and from the growth of income, and therefore the growth of demand arising from other developments.

The generic name for this kind of policy is 'balanced growth' and the first to canvass it was Professor P. Rosenstein-Rodan in a now famous and frequently reprinted article 'The industrialization of East and South-East Europe' (Rosenstein-Rodan, 1943). In this and a subsequent article (Rosenstein-Rodan, 1961), he has argued that the development of manufacturing industries first requires heavy investment in social overhead capital including inland transport, electric power, harbours, a piped water supply and so forth. For technical reasons these forms of investment are indivisible, their minimum size is very large and they therefore require a lot of capital. They also have long gestation periods, i.e. it takes a long time from the moment such a project is initiated until it is completed. To make this heavy investment worthwhile there must be a simultaneous development of producer and consumer goods industries so that the initial excess capacity of the roads, railways and power stations is quickly utilized.

But who is to buy the output of all these new industries? If enough projects are started simultaneously they will generate sufficient income to absorb the increase in supply. The workers in any one industry will spend their (new) incomes on the products of all the other industries. An isolated factory, so the argument runs, may not be able to sell its output since its workers will not wish to spend all their incomes on the one product manufactured in their factory. But if several industries develop simultaneously then Say's Law will apply. Rosenstein-Rodan puts the case aptly: If a hundred workers who were in disguised unemployment in an underdeveloped country were put into a shoe factory, their wages would constitute additional income.

If the newly employed workers spent all of their additional income on shoes they produce, the shoe factory would find a market and would succeed. In fact, however, they would not spend all of their additional income on shoes; there is no 'easy' solution of creating in this way an additional market. The risk of not finding a market reduces the incentive to invest – the shoe factory investment project will probably be abandoned. Let us vary the example: instead of a hundred (unemployed) workers in one shoe factory, let us put ten thousand workers in say one hundred factories (and farms) who between them will produce the bulk of such (wage) goods on which the newly employed workers will spend their wages. What was not true in the case of one single shoe factory will become true for the complementary system of one hundred factories (and farms). The new producers would be each other's customers and would verify Say's Law by creating an additional market. The complementarity of demand would reduce the risk of not finding a market. Reducing such interdependent risks increases naturally the incentive to invest (Rosenstein-Rodan, 1961).

But who will provide all the capital which balanced growth demands? Rosenstein-Rodan recognizes that the low average propensity to save in underdeveloped countries is an obstacle but suggests that the rapid increase in income which a programme of balanced growth would generate will lead to a much higher savings ratio out of the increased incomes. The marginal propensity will thus greatly exceed the average propensity to save.

Balanced growth would, however, require what Rosenstein-Rodan rather inelegantly describes as a 'big push' in the form of government action. Each separate venture taken by itself would fail and would therefore not be attractive to private investors. Only when all are undertaken simultaneously as part of a large-scale investment programme will each project turn out to be a success and lead to an increase in national income. The reason is that each industry bestows external economies on the other.

The term 'external economy' was first used by Marshall to describe the economies which accrue to a firm as a result of the growth of the industry of which it is a part. Thus the growth of the textile industry in England was thought to reduce the individual firm's cost of machinery maintenance by giving rise to specialist firms of repairers, and this was described as an external economy. In the development literature the term has come to take on a different meaning, viz. any external happening which reduces costs to the firm. Thus if the modernization of the fishing fleet provides canners with cheaper fish or a new road reduces transport costs, then this is described as an external economy. It is 'external' because the benefit does not accrue only to the firm or public authority that makes the investment but also to those who benefit from the reduced cost brought about by the investment.

Hence it is said that each industry's money costs will be lowered by the simultaneous development of other industries from which it buys some of its inputs and by the development of an infra-structure which reduces its costs of production. In this way, actual costs will prove to be lower than would have been anticipated by a prospective investor in any one of the industries created. The individual entrepreneur cannot, however, anticipate external economies that will accrue to him and he is therefore certain to underestimate the profit to be earned. But a government which is planning the overall economic development of the country can take the prospective external economies into account and, as it were, 'internalize' them. Consequently, projects which will seem unprofitable to individual entrepreneurs may yet be socially advantageous when several of them are undertaken simultaneously. (Other versions of this balanced growth theory appear in Nurkse, 1953; Lewis, 1955. A sympathetic appraisal is given by Nath, 1962.)

Clearly, a policy of balanced growth on the lines suggested can only be initiated by a government. Further, it is evident that what is envisaged is a large-scale development programme which implies an economic system in which the major decisions about production are taken by a central authority rather than by myriad entrepreneurs each deciding on the basis of whether a project is likely to pay or not. The plea for large-scale state action is not confined to advocates of balanced growth. For example, Professor H. Leibenstein has made out a case for it on the different premise that there is a need for what he calls a 'critical minimum effort' in order that the rate of economic development may exceed the rate of increase of population which, as we shall see later, is above 2 per cent per annum in virtually all underdeveloped countries, and above 3 per cent in some. He argues that it is only when real income per head rises, that people begin to see the advantage of having smaller families so that the growth of population is checked (Leibenstein, 1963, ch. 8). Also, a sharp initial increase in income per head is needed to produce a volume of savings which is adequate for sustained economic growth. A 'big push' is also needed, so it is said, because launching a country into self-sustained growth is like getting an aeroplane off the ground: the aeroplane has to go along the runway at a certain minimum speed, before it will take off (Rostow, 1960).

The arguments for balanced growth and a major breakthrough, or big push, are persuasive but not irrefutable. First, it seems improbable that any underdeveloped country would be likely to have sufficient resources to carry through a programme of balanced growth. To quote one of the critics of such a policy, Professor H. W. Singer, 'the resources required for balanced growth are of such an order of magnitude that a country disposing of such resources would in fact not be underdeveloped' (Singer, 1964, p. 46).

Secondly, those who have treated a policy of balanced growth as synonymous with industrialization – and this specifically excludes W. A. Lewis – have perhaps been inclined to underestimate the problems involved in ensuring an adequate supply of food for those who will no longer be engaged in farming. Unless simultaneous steps are taken to increase the supply of food, its price will rise and that may create damaging inflationary problems resulting from the need to raise urban wages in order to enable urban wage earners to subsist. This can, of course, be interpreted as an argument for balance of a different kind, viz. between the growth of output of manufactures and of food, rather than as an argument against balanced growth as such.

Perhaps the most damaging argument against balanced growth is that, even if it were practicable, it could do no more than create a new, productive, economy which would be superimposed on the existing unproductive economy. It would do nothing to raise the productivity of the pre-existing economy and since experience has shown that large increases in industrial output can be produced with very few workers, the majority of the population would continue to be part of the backward economy. Furthermore, balanced growth seems to be a once for all move, whereas the real object of economic policy ought presumably to be to promote a continuous process of development, not a once for all change.

Professor A. O. Hirschman in a most stimulating book has indeed suggested that, far from balanced growth, what a country should really pursue is a policy of *unbalanced* growth because it is a state of unbalance or disequilibrium which sets in motion the forces which prompt action, and it is action which is needed to obtain economic development (Hirschman, 1958). If there is always perfect balance between demand and supply then there is no incentive to venture on new projects. Like the exponents of balanced growth, Hirschman recognizes the need for state intervention in the economic development of underdeveloped countries, but unlike them his criterion of the success of any particular act of intervention is whether or not it will in turn have further repercussions. He therefore favours projects which have strong 'complementarity effects': take for example the textile and building industries. An expanding building industry will prompt investment in domestic cement production, the making of pre-cast concrete, window frames, glass, and perhaps even structural steel from scrap. By contrast a textile mill will not give rise to anything further and is therefore said to have weak complementarity effects.

Hirschman classifies industries according to whether their expansion will or will not induce further investment in other industries. He does so by introducing the concept of 'forward and backward linkage'. An industry is said to have strong forward linkage effects if it is likely to prompt the setting up of new industries using its output. For example, the setting up of a steel mill – even if it is initially no more than one using only scrap and no iron ore – is likely to give rise to a variety of steel manufactures, such as the making of steel window frames and a variety of simple steel components. Backward linkage occurs when investment in an industry gives rise to further investment in industries that supply it with inputs. Beer brewing, frequently among the first industries to emerge in underdeveloped countries, creates a demand for bottles, and then for bottle tops and eventually crates in which to transport the bottles. Final consumer goods have, by definition, no forward linkages or, at most, relatively weak ones through complementarity whilst agriculture is an example of an industry that has few backward linkages because it uses relatively few inputs, although the increasing use of artificial fertilizers, and pesticides perhaps makes this a bad example, and indeed the coming of the Green Revolution, described in a later chapter, with its demand for tubewell equipment, shows further that the nature of an industry's linkages is not immutable but changes in time. In general, however, it is intermediate industries, rather than primary product or final consumer goods industries which have the most linkages. An iron and steel industry clearly has very strong forward and backward linkages but as Hirschman says 'development . . . cannot be started everywhere with an iron and steel industry just because this industry maximizes linkages' (Hirschman, 1958, p. 108), and indeed, whilst linkage effects are important, no one would suggest the planning of an economy primarily according to linkages.

Linkages cannot be the sole criterion. Often the choice does not in any case lie between promoting Industry A or Industry B but rather which of them to create first. Here again Hirschman offers a strategy by suggesting the most efficient sequence is that which minimizes the time it takes to bring both into existence. Thus the sequence AB is more 'efficient' than BA if by following it B becomes possible sooner than A would have done had the other sequence been chosen.

The notion of efficient sequences need not be confined to the choice between individual industries but can also throw light on the choice of sequence between social overhead capital projects and directly productive activities. It is a mistake to assume that the former must always precede the latter. In practice, of course, governments often have no choice. They may be able to obtain a loan for building a road or a hydroelectric power scheme, but not for setting up consumer goods industries. Conversely, private foreign capital may only be available for particular industries and not for an infrastructure project. For example, many underdeveloped countries have cigarette factories, subsidiaries of one or other of the large international corporations which dominate this field. Their capital would obviously not be available to build roads.

If the attempt at balanced growth is abandoned, what type of industry has the best chance of success in an underdeveloped country? A number of criteria may be used. First, if the aim of developing secondary industries is to raise real per capita incomes in the foreseeable future, as will be assumed here, then one criterion must be the optimum scale of production. Given the typically small market – out of the ninety underdeveloped countries usually listed, seventy-two have less than fifteen million population and fifty-one have less than five million population (Pincus, 1967, p. 66) – industries with a small optimum scale of production have a better chance than e.g. the manufacture of motor cars or synthetic fibres where the optimum scale of production is very large, unless there is a possibility of finding export markets.

Secondly, underdeveloped countries will go for industries that enjoy natural protection through the high cost of importing what is to be produced. This can be either because what is produced is bulky in relation to its value and thus incurs disproportionately high transport charges if imported. Furniture, beer and bricks are typical examples of such industries. Or it may be that the product is fragile, like tableware or glass and therefore more likely to be damaged if imported than if manufactured or assembled domestically. Or there may be products which, like bread and newspapers, are perishable!

The third criterion of selecting an industry is a country's comparative advantage in the relevant field of production. Since, relative to others, underdeveloped countries have generally more labour than capital, this points to the selection of industries that are labour-intensive rather than those which are capital-intensive. But this criterion has been challenged on several grounds. First, it has been argued that underdeveloped countries should, on the contrary, go out of their way to enter new science-based industries because these will have a longer life and are likely to face the highest income elasticities of demand. This school often quotes Professor Gerschenkron with approval.

Gerschenkron has argued that when certain European countries began to industrialize in the latter part of the nineteenth century, the more backward they were the more pronounced was the stress on bigness of both plant and enterprise in their process of industrialization. He also found that the more backward their economies, the more they went for producer goods rather than consumer goods industries (Gerschenkron, 1965, p. 354). He shows that the Russians in the 1890s favoured producer goods industries and therefore, in turn, large capital-intensive plants, because these were the industries that were at that time the technologically most advanced, and Gerschenkron argued that it made sense for a country trying to catch up to choose the industries in which technical advance had been greatest (p. 360). Further, he points out that the low level of final consumers' demand in economically backward countries favours capital goods industries, especially if the Government is prepared to be their customer.

But he did not attempt to turn these findings into a policy

prescription for all underdeveloped countries, and is indeed at pains to point out that the problems facing underdeveloped countries today are different and may require different solutions. Nor does he say that the countries which industrialized in the nineteenth century were right in following the paths they did. As an economic historian his task is to explain *why* one can discern certain trends rather than either to justify or to condemn them. Gerschenkron's work certainly is a great help to an understanding of why several of the present underdeveloped countries display a similar proclivity to favour large-scale projects and producer goods industries, but it does not imply that this proclivity is necessarily well founded.

The past experience of other countries does not in any case provide an unambiguous guide. It is true that in many countries which have experienced a 'take-off into self-sustained growth' – to use Rostow's phrase – it is possible to identify particular industries or sectors which have played a leading role, growing much faster than others, and which have contributed in a decisive fashion to the expansion of others. These industries have ranged from textiles (in Britain but not in other countries) through heavy industry complexes based on railways and military products, to timber pulp, dairy produce and a wide variety of consumer goods. The introduction of railways has probably been the most important single initiator of take-offs. The leading sector has generally employed a relatively advanced technology. At the same time one has also to remember that there have been many instances in which the establishment of a capital intensive industrial nucleus has entirely failed to trigger off a process of growth in the rest of the economy – oil installations in the Middle East, for example, and, some would argue, the heavy industries established in India during the 1950s and early 1960s.

The idea that underdeveloped countries should choose labour intensive industries in line with their comparative advantage has also been challenged on different grounds by Professors Galenson and Leibenstein (1955). They argue the case for capital intensive industries on the grounds that these will make possible a more rapid rate of investment because it will not be necessary to distribute so much income to labour as under a more labour intensive approach. If labour-intensive methods are adopted, more workers will be brought into employment; they will be paid wages and it is unreasonable to expect them to save. Consumption will expand by nearly the full amount paid out in additional wages, and there will be less left over for saving and investment. The argument assumes that the more that is saved and invested the higher will be the rate of economic development and a capital intensive strategy will therefore lead to faster economic development than one in which the share of wages is higher. Galenson and Leibenstein would therefore have countries opt for the strategy of development with the highest 'reinvestment quotient' or one which maximizes productivity per worker minus consumption per worker. In general this predisposes them towards 'heavy' industries in the sense of transport, power and metal-working industries for these tend also to be the capital intensive industries.

Their article includes a table showing, on certain assumptions, the amount of employment provided over a period of time by an initial investment of 1200 rupees in various types of cotton textile machinery. If this sum is invested in hand looms (cottage industry) it will initially provide, on these assumptions, employment for thirty-five people, but there will be no margin for reinvestment and after twenty-five years the number of jobs provided will still be thirty-five. If on the other hand the same sum is invested in a large-scale modern mill, it will initially provide employment for five workers, but, thanks to reinvestment of a large proportion of the income generated (value added), the additional employment will exceed 12,000 after twenty-five years.

These figures run counter to all experience and seem totally unrealistic, as will appear in a later chapter. We have argued before that it is a mistake to assume that 'only capitalists save' and Galenson and Leibenstein's extreme assumptions are therefore inadmissible. Nor is it clear how one can be sure that the entire surplus over and above what is paid in wages will be reinvested, unless one assumes that all investment decisions are taken by the state. Total reinvestment seems the more improbable since their 'model' appears to provide no incentive for it. A strategy in which a higher proportion of value added accrues initially to wage earners and other employees need not be at the expense of reinvestment. Governments can, through appropriate policies, offer incentives to saving and reinvestment. They have a large number of policy instruments at their disposal including taxation, monetary policy and the price policy of state enterprises. But in any case, as was argued earlier, provided investment opportunities exist and are perceived, lack of saving is unlikely to be a stumbling block to their realization except in the most primitive economies. Finally, Galenson and Leibenstein's strategy has implications not only for the distribution of income as between the present and the future, but also for current income distribution as between 'capitalists' and employees which are not likely to gain them much applause. It implies a systematic channelling of all increases in income to 'capitalists' whilst as far as possible preventing the incomes of workers from rising .In a poor country such a policy cannot have much appeal, and can really only be implemented in a totalitarian state.

A more realistic argument in favour of a certain number of capital intensive plants is that they provide training and experience for managers and other employees in modern technology and thereby help to remedy the shortage of experienced and competent industrial managers and workers in underdeveloped countries. It has been increasingly recognized that in this sphere at any rate there is no effective substitute for what is described as 'learning by doing' and this may legitimately weigh in the scales of choice of technique. But to manage a large undertaking is much more difficult than a small one and as a means of disseminating managerial ability and familiarity with machinery, many small enterprises may be more effective than a few large ones.

Perhaps the most cogent objection to development based on capital intensive technologies is that underdeveloped countries simply do not dispose of sufficient capital and cannot conceivably hope to attract enough foreign aid. If a capital intensive technology is chosen then a country can only afford to equip a very small proportion of its labour force with the means of increasing output. One would therefore create small islands of high productivity whilst leaving large parts of the economy untouched.

It is this which has led the search for what is sometimes described as an 'intermediate technology' – neither so advanced that it is beyond the means of underdeveloped countries, nor so primitive as that originally prevailing. The technology embodied in the machines now being produced in the advanced industrial countries is inappropriate because it was developed to economize the use of labour which in the advanced countries is the scarce factor. To use the technology which it has superseded, i.e. the technology used in days when labour was less scarce, is no answer either because that technology was in a sense less efficient. What the underdeveloped countries badly need is equipment which is efficient both in a technical and economic sense. Unfortunately for them, very little effort has been devoted in the machine-making countries to the production of equipment specifically for use in underdeveloped countries because the returns to such effort appear more risky and uncertain than the returns to perfecting machinery for the main machine-using countries of the world. Furthermore, there is a 'market' in the latter whilst the former can only demonstrate a 'need'. Some attempts at designing equipment specifically for underdeveloped countries have indeed been made, especially at the Philips Pilot Plant in Utrecht and under the aegis of the Intermediate Technology Group in London. (Zimmerman, 1965, p. 88).[1] The Japanese have also developed a hand power-tiller for agriculture. Perhaps even more significant have been the instances of adaptation in the low income countries themselves. For example in Northern Nigeria one can see motor cycle engines being used to provide power for very simple grain mills that were originally designed to be hand operated, and there are a number of other examples of new equipment that has

1. See also E. F. Schumacher, *Small is Beautiful*, Sphere Books, 1974.

been pioneered in the underdeveloped countries themselves and some of this would have a market in many other countries facing similar problems, if only they knew of its existence. Maybe, as with the Green Revolution, it is only a matter of time before sufficient resources are put into devising and developing low cost techniques which enhance the productivity of labour without replacing it in the process. And, as with the Green Revolution, a possible source of a major breakthrough will come from one or other of the charitable foundations, like the Rockefeller and Ford Foundations which command the necessary resources for an extended period of development and also have the experience of disseminating its results.

But it is arguable that underdeveloped countries themselves need to lay more emphasis on creating machine-making industries that are responsive to their special needs, viz. that their machines should be technically and economically efficient at lower scales of production than typically prevail in the advanced industrial countries and, secondly, that they should be adapted to the different proportions in which capital and labour are available in underdeveloped countries.

The idea of setting up capital goods industries in underdeveloped countries is often scorned because they are believed to be too highly capital intensive and to require very large markets. But this belief is largely attributable to a natural tendency to think of the steel industry as the prototype of capital goods. One forgets that many of the industries that *use* steel, as distinct from making it, are essentially 'workshops' and use skilled labour much more than capital (Pack and Todaro, 1969; Todaro, 1970). Figures for Japan in 1951 indicate that of twenty-one branches of industry only seven had lower capital output ratios than the machine-making industry (Todaro, 1970, p. 60). Such workshops might not be able to do much to provide alternative technologies for industries like cigarette making in which the machinery is highly specialized, but they would be useful in providing a stimulus and an appropriate technology for the development of small-scale indigenous industries. One could, of course, argue that it is unrealistic to expect that it is feasible to set up such industries just because they are more economical in the use of capital than other industries. There is the difficulty that machine-making requires a variety of skills which are likely to be in short supply, and also that the market for any one type of machine is not likely to be big enough in any but the largest underdeveloped countries. The lack of appropriate skills is however perhaps a strong argument *in favour* of creating machine-making industries for, as was argued earlier, such skills will never come into existence unless there is the opportunity to exercise them. The narrowness of the market can be overcome either by customs unions or by international specialization and trade between groups of underdeveloped countries.

Some of the questions raised in the latter part of this chapter will receive further consideration in the final chapter.

6 Industrial Development

Much that is written about strategies of economic development tacitly assumes that countries start from *tabula rasa*, i.e. that *no* development has so far taken place. In the great majority of countries this is a totally unrealistic assumption to make. Not only have great agricultural export industries come into being like the Ghanaian cocoa industry or Malaysian rubber, but even in the realm of manufacturing a great deal of industry has in fact developed in the last fifty years. To demonstrate this statistically is not easy because listing the number of factories in different countries only makes tedious reading and is also not very instructive except in relation to some yardstick or measure. That is why the degree of industrialization is sometimes measured by the ratio of domestic production of specified goods to the total supply of those goods. By that measure the non-industrial countries are said to manufacture some 70 per cent of their total supply of manufactured consumer goods (GATT, 1959, p. 14). But that is an ambiguous statement if, as is often the case, imports are deliberately restricted, so that total supply would be greater in the absence of such restriction.

The statement is ambiguous in another way: it makes it appear that non-industrial countries are in some sense 'well supplied' with manufactured goods, when in actual fact, because of their poverty, consumption per head of everything is very low.

Nevertheless since most writings ignore past development it may be instructive to say something more about it. In many countries industries have developed that provide a substitute for imports. What follows owes much to an MA dissertation at the University of Sussex by R. Kaplinsky (1970). Import substitution has been both an occurrence and a policy. It has been an occurrence in that anyone thinking of producing something is likely in the first instance to look at the domestic market and to use the current volume of imports as an indication of the demand for a product. But in addition, governments anxious to promote industrial development have systematically examined the feasibility of producing at home what was previously imported and have often offered tariff protection and quantitative import control to encourage infant industries.

Until a few years ago import substitution was seen as virtually the only avenue to industrialization and this was powerfully encouraged by Lewis's influential study (1953) in which he showed how to use import statistics to ferret out feasible industries.

Import substitution has created much inefficiency. Protected from foreign competition and often from competition at home as well, industries have developed which could not hope to compete in world markets. In some the import of capital and intermediate goods has resulted in foreign currency costs as high and sometimes in excess of the savings made on the imports of finished goods. A policy of import substitution has also often been associated with a proliferation of administrative controls and drastic intervention in the economy which have dampened rather than encouraged initiative, and which have diverted the energies of businessmen from reducing costs to negotiating with officials over necessary licences or import permits.

Countries have not been unaided in their drive to industrialization. Often international firms have been eager to set up plants either because they were afraid that unless they did, some competitor would pre-empt the field, or because they were positively obliged to do so by a high tariff wall erected for precisely that purpose. Given the objective of pre-empting the field it is common experience that plants which are established are far larger than the market is likely to warrant for many years. This is intended to act as a deterrent to potential competitors. Such a case is well described in relation to the rivalry between the Michelin and Dunlop tyre companies in Peter Kilby's book on industrialization in Nigeria (Kilby, 1969, p. 74).

Many of the multinational firms that have greatly contributed to industrialization are oligopolies and their decisions when and where to invest make sense only when one remembers that. Thus it is, again, common experience to have great spurts of activity so that after decades of importing a given product – say textiles – several plants are suddenly established one after the other. That is largely explicable in terms of the theory of oligopoly with its emphasis on maintaining market shares rather than profit maximization as a principal motive. Kilby estimates that by 1890 Nigeria was importing enough textiles to warrant one factory operating efficiently. But the first textile mill was not established until 1957; eight years later ten mills had come into existence.

There was a time when manufacturers in the industrial countries established branches in underdeveloped countries which were to supply them with tropical raw materials. The Firestone rubber company's plantations in Liberia is an example. But in the last fifteen or twenty years the connection has more often been in the reverse order: subsidiary plants have been established in underdeveloped countries which the parent company has supplied with components from its existing factories. What has then been created has been an assembly plant, putting together parts imported from the industrial countries. In this way a number of motor car assembly plants have been established. A particularly striking example is Cummins diesel project in India (Baranson, 1967), because it brings out a number of features commonly found in industrial projects sponsored by foreign or multinational companies.

Before Cummins established a plant in India in 1961 it had been exporting some 175 diesel engines and parts a year to India. They anticipated a great increase in demand and estimated that by 1967 the Indian market would absorb 2500 units a year. This optimistic market forecast together with import restrictions imposed in 1958 caused them to set up an assembly plant.

The intention was to rely substantially on imported components in the first instance, but gradually to manufacture the components themselves in India as the market expanded. The Indian firm was not a wholly owned subsidiary but was partly owned by Indian businesses some of which had formerly acted as distributors of the imported engines, and which therefore brought with them knowledge of local conditions and markets as well as ensuring that the enterprise would not be regarded as wholly foreign. Here was a tariff-jumping, market pre-empting venture *par excellence*. Unfortunately the market forecast proved to have been in excess of actual demand by a factor of no less than five (500 engines being sold in 1967) and the cost of production, not unnaturally, proved to be three times as high as in the American parent plant. But gross miscalculation apart the underlying idea of such development has within it the essence of a perfectly sensible strategy, especially if the company also uses the opportunity of lower labour costs in the underdeveloped country to go on to manufacture components for sale to the parent company in the industrial country.

The Cummins project was a failure but it was not a fraud. The same cannot unfortunately be said of all foreign-induced industrial projects. Thus the capitals of underdeveloped countries have sometimes swarmed with smart peddlers of machinery who have offered governments or semi-official development agencies apparently attractive terms or who have bribed ministers and key officials. But whilst most development economists have come across instances of this kind the sum total of fraudulent projects is probably quite small, not least because bribes are not nearly so often accepted as they are offered.

Projects of this kind are not to be confused with 'turn key' projects of a perfectly reputable kind where a foreign Government or enterprise agrees to erect a sophisticated plant and hand over the key to the recipient Government or consortium when the plant is ready for operation. Several Indian steel mills have come into being in this way. Sometimes the donor country also agrees to supply staff for the first few years on the understanding that they would train local counterparts who would take over their jobs in due course. Here the only objection is that at the end of it all, the recipient country still does not know how to set up – say – a steel mill, and in the long-run knowing how to do that may prove to be more valuable than having the mill. 'Give a man a fish and you feed him for a day: teach him to fish and you feed him for a lifetime'. Germany after 1945 quickly reconstructed her shattered industries because the *human* capital, the knowledge how to do things, was still intact. Ultimately economic development must be self-sustained if it is to continue, and in that process the knowledge how to do things is more important than the amount of physical capital in existence.

We have seen that industrialization has been promoted by the offer of tariff protection to prospective industrialists. Sometimes these tariffs have seemed more modest than they really were: one has to distinguish here between a so-called 'nominal' tariff, which is simply the import duty expressed as a percentage of the domestic value of the import and an 'effective' tariff which expresses the nominal import duty as a percentage of the value added. By domestic value added we mean here the difference between the price at which a good is sold and the cost of the components imported from abroad. The 'effective' tariff measures the extent to which the value added of domestic producers can exceed the value added at which they would need to operate to be competitive in the absence of the tariff. It therefore measures the degree of inefficiency which the tariff protects. Suppose a car could be imported for £1000 but was subject to a 30 per cent *ad valorem* import duty, thus making its selling price £1300. Now suppose that it is decided to assemble the car domestically from imported components and that these are allowed to enter the country duty free. If the imported components cost £600, then the assembly plant can incur costs up to £700 on wages, interest and profits ('value added') and still remain competitive with the imported car. In the absence of the 30 per cent *ad valorem* duty it would only have been possible to assemble the car domestically if it could have been done profitably for £400 or less. The duty therefore gives the domestic industry up to £300 protection on £400 value added. A nominal tariff of 30 per cent thus gives 'effective' protection of 75 per cent (cf. Johnson, 1966, p. 13).

It is, of course, not necessary to assume, as we have done, that imported components enter duty free or that all the components are necessarily imported but these assumptions greatly simplify the exposition of the difference between nominal and effective tariffs. If components are liable to import duty the difference between the nominal and effective tariff is correspondingly reduced. If some components are domestically produced, like raw cotton which the Pakistan textile industry buys at less than world market price, then the difference between nominal and effective tariffs may be correspondingly enhanced.

In Pakistan the following table taken from S. R. Lewis's book, but revised by him to accord with the above definitions, shows the difference between nominal and effective tariffs in three categories of industries.

Table 1 **Average 'nominal' and 'effective' rates of protection in Pakistan, 1963–4**

Industries producing primarily:	*Average nominal protection* %	*Average effective protection* %
Consumer goods	66	285
Intermediate goods	33	150
Investment and related goods	35	425

Source: S. R. Lewis (1969, p. 74).

Generally, the difference between the nominal and effective rate of protection varies inversely with the domestic value added as a percentage of the total price of the good protected. Thus, the smaller the value added, the greater will be the excess of the 'effective' over the nominal protection. The startling difference between the two rates in the case of investment goods is largely explained by the prominence of transport equipment and metal products in this industry group – in both these the domestic value added is very small, because the greater part of the 'final' good produced consists of imported components.

Just as industrialization has sometimes been prompted by the erection of tariff walls designed to induce foreign firms to jump over them and establish manufacturing plants behind them, so it has also sometimes been the almost accidental consequence of the disruption of customary supply lines. For example, both the Great Depression of the early 1930s and the two World Wars deprived non-industrial countries of accustomed imports of manufactures. In the former case because it eroded the export earnings with which they had formerly paid for imports and in the latter, because there were not enough ships to bring them and because the industrial countries had in any case to switch much of their machinery to the production of ammunition. Thus Brazil is often cited as a country in which industrialization was greatly promoted by both World Wars.

Industry benefited by the virtual disappearance of foreign competition, especially the disappearance of products which had been exclusively supplied from abroad. However, not only did many Brazilian manufacturers have the domestic market for themselves, but other countries which had been cut off from former suppliers of industrial goods were turning to Brazil as a new source of supply (Baer, 1965, pp. 16 and 29).

In many instances industrialization 'pays' in the sense that resources devoted to it could not have been more profitably employed in other types of development, either, as in the case of foreign firms which have established branch factories, or that of international lending agencies which have made loans for specific industrial projects, because the funds were not available for other developments; or, because the prospective long-term returns were higher than for competing investment fields. Professor Bruton has argued the latter in the case of Argentina where he says that the policy of promoting import substitute industries during the 'thirties' and after the Second World War, with the help of public funds, was only adopted 'after external circumstances had made it clear that no further growth could be expected from export expansion' (Bruton, 1968, p. 3). But this had the consequence that little was done to enlarge the output of meat, which was almost certainly a mistake: not only was there a marked increase in the domestic demand for meat after the Second World War, but the world market boomed for many years and Argentina, instead of cashing in on the boom, devoted itself to creating import substituting industries many of which continue to incur high costs by world standards and thus to charge a good deal more than the price of competing imports.

So far the discussion has been about industries catering for the home market. But especially those in Latin America have found that the possibilities for import substitution are soon exhausted – the 'easy stage' is soon over.

Customs unions have helped to extend the period of import substitution, but it has proved very difficult to form new customs unions or even to maintain existing ones like that of East Africa. The reason is that they tend to bestow unequal benefits on the partners and even if all are better off those who gain least are prone to feel aggrieved. If an import substituting industry is set up in a partner state they not only lose customs revenue but consumers may have to pay more for the product than when it was imported from abroad. Meanwhile the immediate benefits, including new employment opportunities and an increased source of direct tax revenue accrue to the country in which the industry has been established. The fiscal effects of forming a customs union can be to some extent offset by measures of fiscal compensation as was done in East Africa in the early 1960s. But when all countries are eager to have industrial development, none will willingly see new industries go to partner states if there is the slightest possibility that the industry might have been attracted to their own country in the absence of a customs union. These problems are particularly acute when the partners of a customs union are unequally endowed with 'natural' inducements to industry. In East Africa, Kenya on the whole offers a more attractive environment to new industries than either Uganda or Tanzania, and given free choice, new industries depending upon a market greater than any one of the three partners is likely to provide, will generally opt for a Kenya location. No such problem need arise in the case of industries that do not need a market greater than that of any one country because economies of scale are soon exhausted but few industries can operate economically in countries in which both population and *per capita* incomes are small and customs unions might therefore open up possibilities for industrial development that would not otherwise exist (cf. Hazelwood, 1967; Robson, 1968, 1972).

If possibilities of import substitution are exhausted and customs unions offer no further reprieve, then countries must look to export markets for the further expansion of manufacturing. Here the countries that have pursued import substituting policies by protecting industry have placed themselves at a disadvantage in that their industries are too inefficient to compete on world markets. An important recent study undertaken under the auspices of the OECD Development Centre into the industrialization policies of seven major countries in Latin America and Asia recommends a reversal of previous policies (Little, Scitovsky and Scott, 1970). In particular, it urges that administrative controls should be progressively abandoned and that import duties should be reduced to a much lower level where they would serve to raise revenue rather than to protect. Domestic producers should then be taxed at the same level and the combined revenue made available to 'promote' rather than 'protect' industry. Promotional policies might include training allowances or the provision of training facilities and would also include subsidies to wage payments. They argue that unskilled industrial wages are often much higher than the real cost to the economy of employing labour in industry, which is represented by the value of output foregone in non-industrial occupations. As industry becomes more efficient it will be better placed to compete with imports at home and to develop an export trade.

In the search for export industries and export markets the countries that have a longer experience of import substitution industries will of course be competing with others like Hong Kong and Singapore where industrialization has been pursued directly to serve export markets.

For all alike, the existing factor endowments of under-developed countries – especially the lack of people with industrial skills – may seem to suggest that a policy of developing industrial exports is fraught with difficulties. That should not deter them because if it did no new lines of production would ever be developed since, almost, by definition, the factor endowments will be wrong. What one needs to take into account are not the present factor endowments but how easy or difficult it is likely to be to change them. Industrial skills cannot be implanted in the absence of industrialization since they must be, at least in part, learnt 'on the job'. Some, like reasonable punctuality and a capacity to keep regular hours cannot be taught at all except in a context of urban employment, though it need not necessarily be industrial employment.

The development of an export trade in manufactures has many advantages for low income countries. The possibilities of expanding sales may be greater than with primary products. Like the export of primary products, it provides foreign exchange with which to import machinery that cannot be made at home. Foreign exchange is also needed because, given the relatively high marginal propensity to import of countries that produce only a small range of consumer goods, every success in raising incomes will lead to an increase in the demand for foreign exchange. Countries that have difficulty in raising the domestic supply of food may even need foreign exchange to satisfy the growth in the demand for food.

There are always considerable unexploited possibilities of export oriented activities as the recent experience of a number of countries has shown. Countries that export timber have advanced from being producers of logs to being producers of sawnwoods, yet half of the import into Europe of tropical timber continues to be in the form of logs, although the sawnwood imports are now growing twice as fast as imports of logs (Jacobson, 1969). Malaysia has developed a thriving tunafish canning and freezing industry and Hong Kong exports large quantities of textiles, plastic goods, transistors and wigs.

An important recently published book by Lary (1968), has identified manufactured goods in which a labour abundant developing country is likely to have a comparative advantage. He confined himself to products which were actually being exported and whose export were worth at least $100,000 to the exporting country in 1965. Arguing that underdeveloped countries were likely to be relatively short of both capital and skilled labour he arranged products in an order determined by the proportion of value added that accrued to profits (taken as a proxy for the remuneration of capital) and skilled labour. The higher the proportion of value added that accrued to unskilled labour, the more likely it was to have a comparative advantage in developing countries, provided only that their wage rates were not too much above the opportunity cost of labour. On the basis of these two criteria – low skill and capital intensity and at least *some* success in existing export markets – Lary identified numbers of industries that seemed especially suitable. Naturally, they include textiles and clothing in which a number of Asian countries have been so successful. But they also include a wide array of others – automobile parts, pipe fittings, furniture, footwear, glassware, china, pottery, optical goods, watches and printed matter. Having identified the products Lary then points to certain salient features.

1. The trade is at present very small: it accounts for only 13·5 per cent of the developed countries' imports of these goods.

2. Much of this trade originates in a small number of underdeveloped countries, Hong Kong alone accounted for 28 per cent and altogether the Far East supplied two thirds of it.

3. The trade is concentrated in another sense. 45 per cent was accounted for by textiles and clothing; 72 per cent of it went to the USA, Germany and the UK.

4. Exports of these goods have increased by around 13 per

cent annually or about twice as fast as exports of basic commodities.

It would be wrong to imagine that all developing countries could immediately emulate the remarkable success of Hong Kong which was in part due to very special circumstances, not least the inflow of experienced industrialists from mainland China after the new regime came into being, and the inflow of capital from the Chinese all over South East Asia because they preferred their savings to go where they could correspond in Chinese. Indeed, another way in which this export trade is concentrated is that in the other countries of the Far East from which it originates it is predominantly Chinese businesses that have developed it. We saw earlier that deviant ethnic groups have often played a role in economic development out of all proportion to their number, but the point to note here is that the benefits of the enterprise of Chinese businessmen are by no means confined to them. Taken at the lowest, the trade enlarges the country's foreign exchange earnings; it enhances taxable capacity and, given that the prime characteristic of Lary's industries is their labour intensity, it also creates employment and thus distributes income. There is no special reason why what has been accomplished by the Chinese should not be equally possible for Indians, Africans or Latin Americans. All development will afterwards be seen to have been the result of special circumstances. What makes them special is not their existence but that they were perceived and acted upon.

Global figures that show that only 6 per cent of the export of manufactures have their origin in the non-industrialized countries obscure what has happened in particular countries or industries, and yet it is the study of circumstances in which an export trade in manufactures has been successfully developed that is instructive. It is easily forgotten that half India's exports now take the form of manufactured goods or that Kamba woodcarvings make a significant contribution to Kenya's exports. The latter is especially interesting in that virtually no machinery is employed so that the value added accrues directly to large numbers of carvers and traders. Success is partly to be ascribed to ingenuity and considerable business acumen, and partly to the fact that curios have a very high income elasticity of demand in the importing countries (Elkan, 1958). Greetings cards have also enjoyed rapidly increasing sales in Europe and America but so far no under-developed country seems to have taken advantage of the obvious opportunity that this must present to many of them.

It is also worth remembering that success need not necessarily depend upon an increase in total world demand for the kind of goods to be exported. A low income country may be able to produce them at lower cost and thus displace the present high cost suppliers in the older industrial countries. This is what the textile industries of India and Hong Kong have done. That is, however, dependent upon a willingness on the part of the older industrial countries to permit competition with their own industries, and on the whole the industrial countries have been loath to do this. Established high cost manufacturers have persuaded their governments that foreign competition was 'unfair' being based on 'oriental standards of living unacceptable to their own workers' and that their competitors engaged in 'dumping'. These are all phrases highly charged with emotion. The industrial countries are much better placed to move resources out of the kind of industries that low income countries can develop and into the newer science based industries, than are the under-developed countries. Indeed Britain has a better record of permitting, for example, its cotton textile industry to contract than most other industrial countries. But even Britain has at times negotiated invidious agreements with Hong Kong, India and Pakistan under which they themselves were obliged to restrict their exports of textiles to Britain in return for an undertaking that import duties would not be raised. Most of the older industrial countries do now accept the principle of liberalizing the import of manufactures from low income countries, as a way of helping their development, but they are slow to implement the removal of barriers.

7 Agricultural Advance

Poverty, the growth of population and the increasing numbers who live in towns all call for increases in the output of agriculture. So in some cases does the possibility of raising export earnings by selling more of a crop abroad. As we saw earlier, the demand for agricultural primary products in the advanced industrial countries is increasing very slowly but such aggregate considerations are irrelevant to the question of what some *one* country should do in given circumstances. A crop disease in one country gives another the opportunity to corner its market. A slow rise in the demand for raw cotton may still hold out excellent prospects for the country that is able to grow a particular type, like long-staple cotton, the demand for which is distinct from the demand for the commodity in general.

In England in the nineteenth century the growing demand for food was met by imports purchased from America and elsewhere in return for exported manufactures. This solution is not possible for the present low income countries and all must seek to increase output. There clearly is scope for *some* international trade in foodstuffs between underdeveloped countries as witness Kenya's export of temperate products to her neighbouring countries in the tropics, but also the thriving export of Burmese rice to India before the Second World War; but if the factor endowments in neighbouring countries are very similar there is not much scope for trade in food. Food can be and has been imported from advanced industrial countries, e.g. wheat from the USA, but since most of the importing countries are seriously short of foreign exchange this way of augmenting the domestic food supply only makes sense in exceptional circumstances.

If the supply of food fails to rise in proportion to the increase in demand, food prices will rise and this can seriously jeopardize the prospects of non-agricultural development. A rise in food prices will raise wages outside agriculture. This could lead to either a fall in employment or a slowing down of industrial development or both. In any case most low income countries have food deficiencies to start off with in the sense of inadequate calorific intake or an insufficiency of protein and vitamins, so that one reason for wanting to grow more food is to raise the general standard of nutrition.

The UN Food and Agricultural Organization (FAO) has estimated that in underdeveloped countries the intake of calories per person per day is of the order of 2150 compared with 3060 in the high income countries. Protein consumption is 60 grammes compared with 90 grammes, and whereas in the high income countries half the protein consumed is animal protein, in the low income countries animal protein accounts for only one sixth. These figures are averages for some 2500 million people estimated to live in underdeveloped countries (Lowry, 1970). There is, however, a wide dispersion around the mean and in India and Bangladesh, the diet of many people is well below the average. Diets also lack other important constituents such as vegetables and fruit to provide essential vitamins. Dietary deficiencies are largely the result of poverty but are sometimes accentuated by customs and taboos. In parts of East Africa women may not eat eggs and some fish is taboo for men and women alike. Hindus may not eat cow's meat.

Family budget surveys have also sometimes created the impression that even in the poorest countries food in general, and particular items, have low income elasticities of demand. From that it has been inferred that malnutrition has been exaggerated. These consoling findings are largely irrelevant. Budget surveys are almost invariably confined to town-dwellers and often to those in regular employment – a very small and untypical minority. Even they may have a low income elasticity of demand for food – not because they might not like to have more or different food but rather because they are under strong social pressure to spend on other things.

Agricultural output is raised either by extending the area under cultivation or by producing more per acre. It is often said that in the densely populated countries like India or Jamaica no further extension of cultivation is possible. In some parts of these countries that must be true. For example in Mauritius there seems hardly an inch that is not cultivated; each year the sugar cane has seemed to encroach yet further on the narrow roads until there is practically no footpath left at either side of the tarmac. But even in India the area of cultivation has in fact been extended in the last twenty years. Extension of cultivation is largely a function of price. Areas which are not worth cultivating when prices of farm produce are low become economic at higher prices. Sometimes the relationship is indirect: a stretch of land is said to be un-cultivable because it is swamp or infested with tsetse fly or excessively dry or excessively steep. But when produce prices rise it pays to do something about it: swamps are drained, dry land is irrigated and steep slopes are terraced. It does not therefore, make a great deal of sense to divide the earth's surface into that which is cultivable and that which is not as is sometimes done. The area of cultivable land is very much a function of price.

Problems of increasing the output of agriculture are well illustrated by Indian experience.[1] It is generally recognized that until recently Indian agricultural output increased much too slowly in relation to the growth in the demand for it. From 1950, the first year of the First Plan until 1964–5 total agricultural production measured at 1960–61 prices rose at the rate of 3 per cent per year. Foodgrain production which accounts for about two thirds of total agricultural production, rose by 2·8 per cent whilst for other crops, including tea, coffee and sugar cane, the increase was 4·8 per cent. This growth of production fell short of the needs for self-sufficiency in food grains and in 1965–6 8 per cent of available foodgrains were still imported, mostly wheat from the USA under PL 480 which was made available free of charge although the trans-

1. What follows is closely based on Chaudhuri's excellent account of Indian economic development since 1950 (Chaudhuri, 1971, pp. 46–59).

port costs had to be paid for in scarce foreign currency. In the years 1965–7 there was a disastrous fall in output due to the failure of the monsoon but since then output has increased much more rapidly. The increases in the 1950s were attributable partly to increases in the area sown and to a slightly greater degree to increases in productivity (output per acre). But in most recent years there have been much more marked increases in productivity especially of wheat and to a lesser extent of rice. These are described as the Green Revolution and are attributed to the 'new agricultural strategy'. The increases in yield mark an important technological breakthrough. To what extent it has made the food problem in India a thing of the past remains to be seen since it is not yet clear how easy it will prove to extend the area of controlled irrigation and water availability on which the success of the Green Revolution is critically dependent.

Although agricultural production as a whole has increased steadily albeit very slowly over the past two decades there have been very marked differences between the various states, with Punjab in the forefront of advance and Assam and West Bengal at the other extreme.

Many have attributed the slow growth of agricultural output to the low priority which is said to have been given to agriculture by the Indian planners. Although the Plans pay repeated lip service to agriculture, direct expenditure on agriculture in the first three plans is said to have been rather small; further, agricultural prices were deliberately kept down and consequently farmers had no incentive to increase output; and, thirdly, it is alleged that land reform was not pursued with sufficient vigour.

It is true that as a proportion of total expenditure, Agriculture and Community Development declined from 15 per cent in the First Plan to 12 per cent in the Second and 13 per cent in the Third Plan, although in terms of actual expenditure the amount has steadily increased. But as Chaudhuri points out, the benefit from, for example, irrigation projects in one period continue to accrue in the next without any further expenditure and much of the early expenditure was on just that. One has also to remember that farmers themselves devote resources to improving the productivity of their farms and that official development expenditure on agriculture is only part of a total which is usually underestimated because of the intrinsic difficulties of measuring the capital formation of small cultivators. Finally, when a cement works or a steel mill is built the effect on agriculture will depend on what is done with the output. If the cement is used to build grain stores and the steel to build fertilizer plants then it must be reckoned as ultimately contributing to agricultural development.

Nor is there any certainty that greater expenditure on agriculture would necessarily have made a corresponding difference to output before the technological breakthrough of the mid 1960s. One would have to assume that if more had been spent on research earlier the new strains of wheat and rice would have become available sooner and this cannot at all be taken for granted. Besides, since one merit of the new strains is that they respond well to fertilizers they could not have been extensively used until the domestic capacity to produce fertilizers had been created. It also takes time – and not just months – to create an organizational framework that is capable of extending the use of the new techniques over the whole country. Nothing is so difficult as to create routine extension procedures in agriculture where soil and climate differ from place to place and the correct amounts of fertilizer, pesticide, as also the right time for sowing and the right rotations, have to be worked out afresh for every zone or district.

The second criticism levelled against the 'planners' is that by keeping food prices low they discouraged the growth of output, especially of wheat. American wheat obtained under PL 480 was sold in the towns at prices with which Indian farmers could not compete. There has been much argument between economists as to whether this was in fact the case, but the difficulty of choosing a right price for food is by no means confined to India. On one hand governments and urban employers are anxious to keep down wages and are aware that when wages are low to start with any increase in food prices, and therefore the cost of living of employees, is bound to result in rising wages. The early nineteenth century campaign in England for the repeal of import duties on corn was inspired by precisely the same consideration. On the other hand there is much evidence, as we saw earlier, that farmers respond positively to rising prices, and policies to prevent rising prices must be presumed to inhibit a potential growth of production.

The third explanation for the slow growth of output is that despite two decades of legislation to reform the terms on which land can be held and to fix maximum rents, tenant farmers continue to lack security of tenure and to be prone to have their rents raised if it appears to landlords that they could afford a higher rent. The facts are not much in dispute. What is uncertain is whether insecurity of tenure and the fear of rising rents really do or do not deter farmers from raising output if a higher output appears to promise substantially higher incomes. It is too early to ascertain how these factors have operated in areas that have experienced the 'new agricultural strategy'.

The Green Revolution in West Pakistan

Nowhere has there been a more striking increase in agricultural output than in West Pakistan, and it is in relation to West Pakistan that the term 'Green Revolution' is most often used, although some of the increase in output occurred before the new dwarf varieties of rice and wheat (developed under the sponsorship of the Rockefeller and Ford Foundations in the Philippines and Mexico) had come into use (Pearson, 1969).

The successful use of the new seeds requires high applications of fertilizer and an ample but well controlled supply of water. It is therefore readily understandable that the new seeds should have been adopted most rapidly in the Punjab and Lower Indus Region which had been irrigated for over a century, rather than in regions in which farming relied upon rainfall. But the type of irrigation most suitable was the tube-well, because its water supply was more controllable than that emanating from the older river irrigation schemes. These older schemes were in any case primarily designed as a defence against drought. Their purpose was to prevent crop failure, not to maximize crop yields. A small amount of water was spread thinly over a large land area. This was unsuitable for the new agricultural technology and the Green Revolution in West Pakistan was therefore closely associated with a very rapid spread of tubewells (Brown, 1970, p. 25). Farmers in this region have long been accustomed to growing crops on irrigated land and cash crop farming has always been important. Tubewells were originally introduced to reduce the underground water level which had been rising dangerously as the result of prolonged large-scale irrigation without which this area would have been largely arid. The technicalities of irrigation need not concern us here. Suffice it to say that when the underground water table rises, it eventually stifles the roots of crops and turns good agricultural land into waste. At the same time a rise of the water-table is not incompatible with a water shortage for agriculture. If, for part of the year the irrigation canals are dry and if, even when they carry water, it is insufficient for all the land on which crops could be grown so that a part of the land has to be left fallow, other land which, given water, could yield two or even three harvests a year, yields only one.

The introduction of tubewells was therefore originally intended merely to reclaim land that had been turned into waste, but proved to have the incidental advantage of providing farmers with a greatly increased and easily controllable supply of water at all times of the year. It was this which made possible the introduction of new seeds known to respond well to fertilizers but which only worked provided there was an ample, but controllable, supply of water. The first power-driven tubewells were established by the Government, but what makes the story of agriculture in the 1960s so remarkable is the speed with which farmers recognized the advantages of tubewell irrigation, and with which they themselves had such tubewells installed on their farms. In recent years the rate of installation has risen to 10,000 a year and virtually all of them have been paid for by farmers, not the Government. The amount of irrigation water increased by 50 per cent between

1960 and 1970 mostly as the result of private tubewell development (Nulty, 1972, pp. 54–6). At first, in the late 1950s, tubewells followed the extension of the electricity grid. The high water level combined with the availability of electric power made the installation of power-driven tubewells especially cheap. But so high were the returns to this investment that farmers away from the grid quickly followed their example even though the private capital cost was enhanced by the need to install diesel engines to run them. The reason is not far to seek. Mrs Nulty has estimated that by installing tubewells and adopting a new farm 'technology' involving the use of artificial fertilizers, farmers could increase their *net* farm income by as much as 100 per cent (Nulty, 1972, p. 81). The payback period for a tubewell that may have cost rs 10,000 is often no more than one or two years.

Most observers have attributed the rapid spread of tubewells and of the new technology involving greater inputs of fertilizer and the new seed varieties to a Government policy change in the mid 1960s which permitted a substantial rise in the price of food crops (Bose and Clark, 1969). Food prices had been held down previously, just as in India, in the interest of town-dwellers – or at any rate their employers. But if Mrs Nulty's findings about the profitability of the new technology are well founded, then we may also accept her statement that 'price effects have had only a minor, if any, part in the rate of growth of agricultural output over the last fifteen years . . . the new technology raises productivity in agriculture so much, that over a wide range it would not be true to say that prices of agricultural commodities determine the attractiveness of investment in new techniques' (Nulty, 1972, p. 92). Pakistan's experience would, however, then be exceptional (Wharton, 1969). In most underdeveloped countries it has often taken substantial increases in price to induce farmers to change their method of production or to grow new crops, and whatever the case in West Pakistan, this is important to remember, because non-economists are too prone to ignore price effects and to attribute what they describe as 'peasant conservatism' to an unwillingness on the part of farmers to take risks which, even if justified by events, provide only marginal increases in income. A farmer not far from the margin of subsistence and often without reserves on which to fall back if the harvest fails is bound to be more concerned to avert risks than to maximize expected profits. That is why major changes in peasant agriculture have been invariably associated either with sudden large increases in the price of one or more agricultural product, or with a technological innovation which yields very large returns. This no doubt explains why even in West Pakistan it has been noted that the smallest farmers have not availed themselves of the new techniques, and it has been mostly the middle-size and larger farmers who have adopted them (Wharton, 1969). Only when the prospective profits substantially outweigh the risks of failure will peasant farmers take the risk of abandoning long established practices which have sometimes been evolved over centuries because they were found to have one major advantage: they minimized the risk of harvest failure due to crop disease or the vagaries of the weather or, as in Mauritius, the possibility of a tornado.

Because farmers need large inducements to take risks it does not follow that they have a 'backward sloping supply curve'; nor does it follow that having taken the leap and successfully raised their incomes to a higher plateau, a fall in price will immediately cause them to reduce production. Something like the 'ratchet effect' which is said to operate in advanced industrial countries operates equally among the rest of mankind. Having become accustomed to a certain standard of life, a fall in the price of their crops will cause small farmers to grow more not less, for that is their only hope of maintaining their customary income.

The West Pakistan Green Revolution yields other important lessons for agricultural development. First, the new technology not only produces a much higher output per man but can also lead to an increase in employment in agriculture, as well as bringing more land into production. The increase in employment takes place because more land can be cultivated and the higher yielding seeds require more labour in preparing the seed beds, applying fertilizer, weeding, applying pesticides, harvesting and threshing. More labour is also needed because the new techniques permit double or even treble cropping. It takes the form partly of the fuller utilization of a previously underutilized labour force and partly of the increased employment of outside labour. In northern India the increase in demand for labour during the harvesting season was such as to cause serious labour shortages and resulted in substantial increases in wage rates (Brown, 1970, p. 104). In Japan and Taiwan large increases in yield were obtained on small farms without resort to the introduction of tractors. In West Pakistan there has been a rapid introduction of tractors because the larger farmers found that in the face of higher labour costs it paid to substitute tractors. But this was only because of a sharp divergence between private and social cost. Farmers were able to buy imported tractors duty free at a greatly over-valued rate of exchange which actually made them cheaper than in the country of origin. Consequently employment has increased less than it would otherwise have done and the import of tractors has wasted valuable foreign exchange (Bose and Clark, 1969). But tractors can also *augment* the supply of labour at critical times in the agricultural year when land needs to be ploughed as fast as possible and when the area of land that can be cultivated is determined by how much ground can be prepared in a limited period. In much of Southern Asia tractors compete with draught animals rather than with labour and they have the advantage over draught animals of not using precious crops as fodder.

Tractors are in fact more versatile than bullocks and although bullocks have been traditionally used to draw carts, tractors do it more speedily and efficiently and can even be used to drive a grain mill or a pump. Against these advantages the bullock, of course, provides manure as a 'joint product', is less prone to irreparable breakdown at crucial junctures, and does not draw on scarce foreign exchange.

Secondly, the demand for tubewells has given rise to an entirely new and important industry. At first the tubes and associated gear were imported. But locally made ones soon began to appear and although technically less efficient at first, they could be obtained more quickly by farmers eager to go over to the new farming system. 'Indeed', writes Mrs Nulty

one of the most remarkable and important aspects of private tube-well development in West Pakistan has been the strong linkage between agriculture and small-scale industry dispersed away from longer established urban industrial centres. In the last decade entire towns and sections of towns have grown and developed almost entirely around the domestic manufacture of diesel engines for private tubewells, other tubewell parts, and, of course, the drilling, installation and repair operations. The agricultural investment in private tubewells has encouraged additional investment in small-scale manufacturing, very little of which actually gets measured for national accounts purposes (Nulty, 1972, p. 103).

Thirdly, the Green Revolution in Pakistan sheds interesting light on the role of Government in promoting agricultural development. It is usually said that increased productivity on peasant farms will only occur after long research, generous subsidies to farmers, credit facilities and very labour intensive extension work needed to persuade farmers to adopt new techniques. In West Pakistan tubewells and chemical fertilizers have been disseminated almost entirely by private example, and the supply of new inputs has not yet caught up with the demand (Nulty, 1972, p. 198). But West Pakistan and northern India are in many ways very untypical of peasant farmlands as a whole. Farms are larger – certainly those that were quickest to go over to the new methods – and farmers had long been accustomed to growing crops for the market on irrigated land. There was therefore, no new complex method to be learnt, except how to use artificial fertilizers and pesticides, and a commercial system of middlemen had been in existence for a century linking growers with consumers both in rural and urban areas. Technical considerations also favoured West Pakistan and northern India: the new wheat and rice seeds are unsuitable even for Bangladesh and Assam because they do not work where skies are often overcast and where the fields are flooded for long stretches at a time. Indeed traditional rice growing in Bangladesh takes advantage of the fact that it has one of the highest rates of rainfall in the world and the paddy is grown in flooded fields. The new varieties would need heavy preliminary investment in flood control. In the Punjab that is unnecessary and indeed it has the advantage of a high water table so that the tubewells do not even have to go very deep: elsewhere they may need to go much deeper (Brown, 1970, p. 80).

But quite apart from these technical considerations the economic landscape of West Pakistan and northern India is unusual. Farmers were not as poor even before the great increases in their incomes, and literacy is said to be more widespread. The Green Revolution is solving India's and Pakistan's food problem in the sense of liberating them from a dependence on imports. But it is not yet clear how the potential increases in output in one relatively small part of the country can be sold in other parts where incomes have not risen because the productivity of agriculture has not increased. For the moment the surpluses of northern India and West Pakistan have replaced imports and there has also been a diversification of crops, with increases in the production of fruit and vegetables. There is also scope for much greater livestock production which in common with fruit and vegetables faces a higher income elasticity of demand than wheat and rice. But the poverty of Bangladesh and Assam is not soluble by agricultural advances in a neighbouring region, and the Pearson Report, by focusing attention exclusively on what can be achieved technically and economically to augment aggregate supply, has failed to address itself to the problem of its distribution.

This problem becomes particularly intractable when it is associated with great regional disparities, as is nearly always the case in poor countries. We are accustomed to the idea that industrial development creates regional disparities since it cannot occur everywhere simultaneously.

Myrdal's analysis showing that equilibrating mechanisms work only very imperfectly, and that regional disparities become greater not smaller as industrial development proceeds, applies with even greater force when the development is agricultural. In the case of industrial development there is always the possibility, however weak, that its increasing demand for labour, food and agricultural raw materials will have 'spread effects' which benefit the rest of the country. In agricultural development these spread effects are even weaker. Even when it gives rise to associated activities outside agriculture these still tend to be localized and unless there are marked differences in the comparative advantage of growing particular crops which would create the necessary conditions for interregional trade, the sole spread effect would be an increase in the demand for labour leading to interregional migration. There are instances of such migration; for example, that of the Banyaruanda from Rwanda and Burundi to the cotton and coffee farms of Central Uganda. But if there is a labour surplus to start with, agricultural development will not give rise to employment opportunities for people from other regions, and the problem of how to improve the standard of life including the level of nutrition in the other regions, remains unsolved.

8 Growth of Population

It is well known that the population of the world is increasing faster than ever before and that the present, rapid rate of growth is a very recent phenomenon, going back no more than twenty years or so. Although some of the industrial countries have also seen an increase in the rate of population growth this has been only exceptionally by as much as 2 per cent per year, whilst in the underdeveloped countries the rate of increase has been almost uniformly at rates of 2 per cent or more. By the mid-60s it was rising typically by 2·5 per cent whilst in some countries the increase was proceeding at a rate of 3 per cent and even higher. If present rates were to continue then the population of India, for instance, which was some 430 million in 1960 would rise to over 900 million by the end of the century and that of Tanzania would increase from ten million to thirty-six million over the same period.

What has unleashed the great demographic acceleration in the underdeveloped countries has been a rather sudden and continued drop in mortality after the Second World War. Since the crude death rate is influenced by the age structure the fall in mortality is better measured by the life expectancy at birth which expresses the average length of life of a new born infant under prevailing conditions of mortality. In the Western world the increase in life expectancy was slow and irregular. It was probably 30–35 years in the middle of the eighteenth century; in 1900 it was about fifty years and not until 1940 did it reach sixty-five. In the underdeveloped countries that increase in life expectancy has come about much more quickly. For example in Mexico it rose from thirty-six years to sixty years between 1930 and 1964 and in Mauritius it is thought to have gone from thirty-eight years in 1940 to fifty-eight years in 1960. Taking underdeveloped countries as a whole it has been estimated that the average expectation of life at birth rose from twenty-five years to forty-five years during the twenty years following the end of the Second World War.

The remarkable increase in population in the underdeveloped countries has come about, broadly, as the result of a marked fall in the death rate without any corresponding fall in the birth rate. If, as was not untypical, both birth and death rates were around forty per thousand of the population to start with, and the death rate then fell to fifteen per thousand, this would lead to an increase of the population by twenty-five per thousand or 2·5 per cent. Although these figures are merely illustrative they do in fact correspond to what has happened since the Second World War in many underdeveloped countries, including some of the largest and most densely settled such as India and Pakistan (Ohlin, 1967).

Both the rapid fall in the death rate and the maintenance of the previous high birth rate require explanation. The fall in the death rate has really to be seen as comprising two elements: a lengthening of the life of adults and a fall in infant mortality. The life span of adults is not so very different from what it was before and the fall in the death rate has been particularly concentrated in the first year of life. The rapid rise in population must therefore be seen primarily as a consequence of the fall in infant mortality and to a lesser extent as resulting from a greater expectation of life once the critical first year of life has been survived.

The marked increase in life expectancy at birth cannot be attributed to one 'explanatory variable' alone. Part of it is due to basic economic improvements. More efficient and regular distribution of food has averted food shortages and mitigated famines, and improved nutrition may account for much of the spectacular reduction of infant mortality. But post-war public health measures have also been extremely effective in underdeveloped areas. The eradication of malaria by spraying with insecticides has had spectacular effects in many countries in which malaria was previously both endemic and lethal, especially for children. In Ceylon, where the death rate had already fallen to twenty per thousand, the first major antimalaria campaign with DDT in 1946 coincided with a fall in the death rate from twenty to fourteen per thousand within a year (Newman, 1967, p. 14).

In Ceylon, as in many other countries where similar improvements in the death rate have been recorded, economic conditions have also improved, but in Mauritius where a sharp decline in the death rate has also been attributed to malaria eradication, this occurred in combination with a deterioration of economic conditions.

It would probably not be untrue to say that the actual fall in the death rate can usually be explained as the direct result of public health measures such as the elimination of malaria, but the resulting rise in population could be supported only by increases in food supply. The post-war public health measures were partly a result of the greater world concern for the underdeveloped countries which lay behind the increasing willingness of the industrial countries to provide aid and especially technical assistance, and partly of a technical breakthrough during the Second World War which created a very effective technology for combating the major causes of premature death. It was during the war, when British, Commonwealth and American forces were deployed in large numbers in the tropical countries of the East and Africa that scientists were called upon as a matter of urgency to find ways of protecting these troops. This led to two especially important inventions for the control of malaria; first, the invention of drugs which were much more effective than quinine as prophylactics and as suppressants of the symptoms, and secondly the invention of DDT which proved to be a much more powerful insecticide than pyrethrum. Finally, during and after the war, techniques were evolved, based on DDT, for the permanent eradication of malaria from whole regions or even countries, by a carefully planned campaign of spraying and simultaneous draining of marshy grounds in which the malarial mosquito was known to breed. Better drugs were also developed for the treatment of other tropical diseases and routine procedures were evolved for mass vaccination and inocculation against typhus, cholera and yellow fever.

The improvements in health in the tropical underdeveloped countries owe a great deal to the technical assistance provided by western governments directly or through the UN World Health Organization. The underdeveloped countries had neither the knowledge nor the resources nor the trained personnel to carry out these campaigns unaided. But it is also important to note that the spectacular improvements in health could not have been brought about without the technical innovations that occurred during, and as a consequence of, the Second World War. We can draw an important lesson from this which also bears on agricultural development, as we saw in chapter 7, viz. that it is much easier to find the resources for major advances when appropriate techniques which are manifestly superior have come into existence.

Without this major advance in technology and its application it is improbable that there would have been such a pronounced increase in population, for improvements in economic conditions by themselves were not sufficient to account for them. Indeed, as will appear, the rapid rise in population has probably on balance retarded the rate of economic improvement in many countries.

We have become used to hearing that the rapid growth of population in underdeveloped countries must be arrested if economic development is not to be retarded, and this is almost certainly the case. But before making it, it is also worth drawing attention to the argument advanced by some, including Professor Hirschman (1958), that the growth of population can also act as a stimulus to development. The case *against* rapid population growth in poor countries is that it absorbs large amounts of food and other resources which may otherwise be used either for increased consumption or for development. It would free resources of capital needed to provide a given level of provision of social overhead capital like schools, housing and hospitals for ever larger numbers and make them available for projects which raised social and economic provision per head. But it is also arguable that in the sparsely populated regions of Africa and Latin America a 'thickening' of the population will be a stimulus to development and that even in countries like India or Bangladesh which are densely populated, a rapid growth of numbers will be a powerful inducement to development by providing a challenge. The response to this challenge, so it is sometimes argued, will then go far beyond a mere restoration of the previous balance and thrust the economy forward into growth of real incomes and welfare. This view is put in its most sweeping form by Professor Hicks when he says that 'perhaps the whole Industrial Revolution of the last two hundred years has been nothing else but a vast secular boom largely induced by the unparalleled rise in population' (Hicks, 1939, p. 302), whilst Hirschman argues that 'the qualities of imagination and organization developed in these tasks of *maintaining* standards of living in the face of population pressures are very similar to those that are needed to *increase per capita* incomes' (Hirschman, 1958, p. 177).

The relevance of Hicks' analysis is speculative, to say the least. One has to remember that in the eighteenth and nineteenth centuries population growth in the European countries never exceeded 1·5 per cent and that, in general, the rises in population followed and did not precede the great increases in productivity brought about by technological advance. Hirschman's assertion may be thought by some to be intuitively plausible but it is not susceptible to empirical verification or refutation in any obvious way.

The case *against* the continuation of rapid rates of population growth is better founded. First, since it is largely the result of a reduction of infant mortality it leads immediately to an increase in the 'dependency ratio', i.e. the proportion of the population which is below (and above) the age of being economically active. The higher the proportion of the population under fifteen or over sixty-five, the less there is left to consume for the 'active' population, i.e. those between fifteen and sixty-five years of age. Some also argue that insofar as economic development is dependent upon savings, the more dependants one has the less one can save, but as we saw earlier there is probably not in reality a meaningful link between personal savings as here perceived and the rate of capital formation. Finally, it cannot be disputed that the high proportion of children is unquestionably making it much more difficult to provide school places than would otherwise be the case. Given the importance attached to providing universal education as quickly as possible, the high ratio of children to adults is undoubtedly imposing much greater burdens on society. Fewer children would reduce the amount of public and private expenditure needed to attain a given level of educational provision.

The rate of population growth will decline when people decide to limit births by the adoption of some method of contraception. An initial effect of a reduction in infant mortality is a rise in the size of families as children who had formerly died in infancy now survive. Nineteenth century English families came to be much larger than families had been in earlier centuries, and it was not until the 1880s that some parents began to practise family limitation. They did so in order to be able to give their children a better start in life and in order to take advantage of the rise in real incomes which appears to have begun in the middle of the century and to have accelerated from about 1870 onwards.

There are, however, formidable obstacles to be overcome before family limitation becomes practicable. First, in societies with a high death rate, a high birth rate is necessary for survival. Social sanctions to ensure survival are incorporated in the religious systems of such societies in the form of sanctions against any attempt at artificial family limitation. Religious beliefs often continue even when the reason for them disappears. It is no stranger that orthodox Hindus continue to eschew birth control than that orthodox Jews continue to abstain from eating pork. In practice, however, when ideas or beliefs become manifestly out of date they usually give way much more readily than is often supposed, and social sanctions against birth control have not in practice been a major impediment to its adoption.

Secondly, in low income countries children are an insurance

for old age. In the absence of governmental systems of social insurance who else other than today's children will look after the old? This is especially true in non-monetized societies where it is impossible to save for old age, since crops cannot be hoarded from year to year. As with religious beliefs the idea of rearing as many children as possible to ensure a comfortable old age is not readily abandoned until its absurdity when families get ever larger, becomes manifest.

But it would be distorting history to suggest that in previous ages the birth rate has been as high as the physical ability to have children ('fecundity') permitted. Most societies have at all times exerted some limitation on fertility by various institutions surrounding sex and child birth. The postponement of marriage, permanent celibacy, taboos on sexual intercourse at certain times are among the institutions which have long legitimized restraint on maximum fertility. Most societies have a long history of induced abortion, infanticide and certain forms of contraception (Ohlin, 1967, p. 66).

Successful family limitation, however, may also involve some readily available means of practising birth control. As with agricultural yields and malaria eradication, it was until quite recently the lack of a suitable technique of contraception which retarded the spread of family limitation. This has perhaps been much more important than religious or social sanctions or ideas about old-age insurance. This is borne out by a number of surveys which have been taken in under-developed countries in recent years to discover more directly what attitudes towards birth control actually prevail.

Instead of confirming the notion of vast continents committed by ingrained values to the maintenance of maximum fertility, they have revealed that in all parts of the world parents of many children would prefer to have no more, and that those who have heard of birth control are anxious to know more about it (Ohlin, 1967, p. 11).

It is difficult to be certain about a subject on which people tend to be very reticent. Ohlin suggests that

modern contraceptives were not at first particularly important to the fertility decline in the industrialized countries. Coitus interruptus, abstention and abortion were in all probability the principal means by which couples reduced the number of births. Coitus interruptus seems to have been and probably still remains the most widely used method of preventing conception in all countries of Europe (Ohlin, 1967, p. 67).

But at present in the underdeveloped countries, the only prospect of a substantial reduction in the birth rate seems to be the hope that a deliberate campaign of persuasion coupled with effective provision of a cheap and reliable contraceptive, will prove effective. That is why the invention of the contraceptive pill and even more that of the intra-uterine device (IUD or 'coil') have made such a difference to the prospects of success. The coil in particular has great advantages over other methods of contraception in that it is not only extremely cheap and very reliable, but also has the advantage of not requiring sustained motivation or positive effort. Once inserted, which takes only a minute, it remains permanently in place unless it is removed because parents have decided to have another child. It does however, require skilled fitting and whilst it minimizes the cost to the individual (as compared for example with the use of condoms) its dissemination imposes a cost on society.

An interesting attempt to compare this cost with the benefits likely to be obtained from fewer births was made recently by Enke and Zind (1969). The cost of reducing the birth rate is the expenditure for birth control clinics and staff, the distribution or fitting of contraceptives and campaign publicity. They estimate that the direct cost per couple 'accepting' birth control could vary between $1 to $3 per year, and take the mean $2 as the figure to use in their computation. They assume an initial income per head of $150 and their model of development makes quite reasonable assumptions (in so far as one is at all willing to accept such a model even as a useful first approximation) about savings rates, capital output ratios and ratios of the labour force to the population as a whole. They assume a gradually increasing success in persuading, first, older and then younger women to practise birth control. Their finding is that over a period of twenty-five years the extra income earned by the population which has practised birth control is sixty-five times as great as the cost. Many alternative investments in productive facilities and equipment would do well, they say, if, after twenty-five years by a similar calculation they earned not sixty-five times but four times their cost. 'Hence economic development programmes', they continue, 'may do fifteen or more times better when they invest in slowing population growth rather than in accelerating output growth' (Enke and Zind, 1969, p. 50). Complete birth control is an unattainable ideal. Enke and Zind have assumed a programme proceeding at a steady rate at the end of which half the country's fertile women are practising birth control. At the end of twenty-five years total GNP with the programme is assumed to be slightly smaller than it would otherwise have been because with a smaller labour force less will be produced. But GNP per head which was assumed to be $150 initially, will have risen to $255 with the birth control programme compared with $206 which it would have been without it.

They also compute what would be the total extra output produced by one person during his lifetime – the output that would be foregone if he had not been born – and compare it with what that person would consume in the course of his life. Using a discount rate of 15 per cent (which seems rather high) they calculate that the present value of that person's consumption over his lifetime exceeds what he will produce by nearly $300 or twice the income per head presumed to obtain in the initial year.

They do not, of course, conclude from all this that governments in developing countries should henceforth concentrate exclusively on birth control programmes and cease to invest in productive capital, or in health and education. One reason is that even if half of all fertile women (or their spouses) participated, the annual cost per head of population would only be 30 cents as compared with $10 per head typically spent on economic development in many low income countries – i.e. it would be no more than 3 per cent of Government development expenditure.

To use cost-benefit analysis as a way of determining an optimum population policy has sometimes been questioned. In one sense the arithmetic is bound always to make the benefit exceed the costs. If the benefit of a birth prevented is the sum of the amounts that would have been consumed over his or her lifetime, whilst the cost is the production foregone, then it can be shown that, even ignoring any discounting of future costs and benefits, consumption is likely to exceed production if only because consumption takes place from birth to death whilst production is confined to the period between, say, the age of fifteen and sixty when most men and some women are 'economically active'. If one further assumes that the contribution to output is that of the marginal worker and that his output will therefore be less than the average output of the labour force, it must seem certain that birth prevention will always 'pay'. We have, however, only to drop the last assumption, that the birth prevented is that of the marginal worker, to cast serious doubt on the inevitable efficacy of birth control. Suppose instead that in the early stages birth control will be accepted more readily by the middle classes than by those lower down the social scale, and that over a lifetime middle class children produce more than they consume. Suppose further that in addition, they provide savings which may generate economic development and also entrepreneurship and 'high-level' inputs. In that case – and it is not an unrealistic one – the whole arithmetic may be turned upside down (Leibenstein, 1969).

Whilst it is thus relatively easy to dismiss cost-benefit evaluations of family limitation programmes as no more than persuasive pieces of gadgetry it is more difficult to deny the intuitive case for slowing down the rate of population growth in countries that may never find it easy to raise total GDP by more than 7–8 per cent per annum. One can perhaps also take solace from the fact that in England where, in the 1880s, family limitation undoubtedly began at the apex of the social structure and only gradually trickled down the social scale, the dire consequences for economic growth which these forebodings predict did not in fact ensue.

We saw earlier that one reason for continuing high fertility might be that parents see in large families an assurance that they will be provided for in old age, but the evidence from many countries points to a growing wish to limit the size of families, and given an appropriate technology there is no reason to doubt that this can be done. But it will need much higher levels of government expenditure on family planning – not only on initial campaigns to disseminate knowledge about contraceptive techniques, but also recurring expenditure on the staffing and equipping of clinics. If the required level of expenditure is compared with the savings resulting from fewer births it may appear less daunting than at first sight.

9 Employment and Unemployment

One of the most serious problems facing many underdeveloped countries is that the numbers who need to earn a living appear to be increasing faster than the opportunities for doing so. This could be put more simply by saying that the labour force is growing faster than employment but the term 'employment' needs to be used with the utmost caution in countries where the great majority earn their living, not as 'employees' or wage earners, but by working with their kinsmen on family farms. On these farms it is unusual for people to be employed for wages, although practice varies from country to country and even within countries. Sometimes outsiders are employed temporarily on a casual basis, especially at harvest time and during other peak periods in the agricultural cycle. But in general, wage employment in most underdeveloped countries is a minority status, seldom encompassing so much as 20 per cent of those of working age, and often fewer. Further, it is a shifting 20 per cent in the sense that people often alternate between periods of employment and periods of self-employment or work on the family farm, so that it is easier to think in terms of the number of wage *jobs* at a moment of time than of the number of wage earners.

An increasing labour force, the result of past increases in population, can be accommodated either within the system of family farms and family businesses or in wage employment. The extent to which the former has occurred is very difficult to measure except negatively by saying that anyone not absorbed in wage employment must be presumed to have been accommodated in other ways. It is sometimes taken almost for granted that anyone not absorbed in wage employment must be unemployed and recent writings on underdeveloped countries abound with references to the menace of growing unemployment and with figures purporting to indicate the precise extent especially of urban unemployment. Some of the figures are 'educated guesses' – like that of Professor H. W. Singer who estimates that 'the true unemployment rate in developing countries is, today, of the order of 25 per cent including the unemployment equivalent of clear under-employment, but excluding a good deal of disguised un-employment in the form of unproductive labour' (Singer, 1970, p. 1).

Other figures have been based either on the numbers of registered unemployed at Employment Exchanges or on statistical surveys of the labour force. Let us examine each in turn (for a thorough review of the evidence see Turnham, 1971).

Figures of unemployment based on registration at Employ-ment Exchanges are virtually meaningless for two reasons. First, most vacancies in underdeveloped countries are not notified to the employment exchanges because in a situation of competition for jobs, employers have no difficulty in filling them from applicants who write or call at the door or who have relatives already at work in the firm. Secondly, given that this is well known, few bother to register. It is only in countries in which the state provides unemployment relief pay that there is an inducement to register the fact that one is unemployed, as payment of 'benefit' will be conditional upon registration. Underdeveloped countries cannot afford to provide unemploy-ment relief pay and there is therefore no particular incentive to register. Indeed the registers usually include the names of people who are not unemployed at all but hope that the Employment Exchange might one day come up with a better job. Statistics of unemployment based on registration are therefore best ignored.

Unemployment statistics based on statistical surveys of the labour force suffer from two defects. First they tend to use classifications based on the characteristics of advanced industrial countries in which it may be legitimate to distin-guish sharply between employed and unemployed. But in the underdeveloped countries no such simple classification makes sense because large numbers may consider themselves unemployed even though objectively they are not because in practice they are able to earn a living in what is often misleadingly described as the 'traditional' sector. It includes trades like photography, vehicle repair and running a taxi service none of which one ordinarily associates with the word 'traditional'. Some work in the businesses of relatives, others are traders or hawkers, have market stalls or sell fuel. If they still consider themselves unemployed it is usually because they would prefer a job in a factory or office or Government Department. Such employment, variously described as 'modern sector' or 'enumerated', comes within the orbit of statutory wage regulation or collective agreements between employers and trade unions, and generally pay is higher than in small-scale indigenous businesses. For reasons to be examined, 'enumerated' employment has increased very slowly and since towns have grown rapidly the mistake is often made of deducting the one from the other and treating the difference as unemployed. But that is clearly inadmissible. One would have to suppose that very great numbers are unemployed and totally dependent upon the small number of employees in the enumerated establishments and that accords neither with common sense nor with the experience of trained observers.

There is, however, a second problem about figures of unemployment derived from statistical surveys of the labour force. It is in practice difficult to know what constitutes unemployment in a setting where many of the urban unemployed have alternative opportunities of earning a living on family farms. Many of the job seekers in the towns are young men who have left school. The conventional wisdom is that these school leavers are appalled by the prospect of working on the family farm and of rural boredom and that they are attracted to the towns by the bright lights and a feeling that some years at school make a career in urban wage employment more appropriate than the traditions of the family farm. This is said to explain the widespread phenomenon of 'urban drift'.

Such an explanation ignores the fact that those who succeed in getting an urban job are in fact likely to be better off than those who remain at home. This is partly because, as we shall see, urban wages, especially in Africa, have risen far above the 30 per cent margin over rural incomes which W. Arthur Lewis assumed in his model of development with unlimited supplies of labour. But one has also to put oneself in the position of young school leavers and to consider the actual choices confronting them. If they remained at home it would be several years before they were old enough to be independent farmers and earn an independent income. They may have to wait until they have inherited land and in those societies where much of the work in the fields is done by women they cannot be independent until they are married. Meanwhile, as a member of the parental household they will, of course, have a roof over their head and receive their food. But they will be largely at the mercy of the head of household for any cash that they may receive. By contrast a job in town will provide them with an independent income at once and, moreover, one that is paid regularly instead of being subject to the vagaries of the weather or of world market prices, as farmers' incomes so often are. There is therefore no need to look for extra-economic factors to explain the phenomenon of 'urban drift': whatever the average rural–urban income gap may be, there is clearly nothing irrational in opting for urban employment when one looks at the alternatives confronting prospective job-seekers.

Their families who have paid the school fees may of course also exert pressure on them to get a paid job rather than remain at home. This is a hangover from the days when only a small minority had the opportunity to go to school and anyone with a few years schooling was eagerly sought after by employers and therefore commanded an 'economic rent'. But although employers still give preference to applicants for jobs who have been educated, supply at present wage levels now exceeds demand.

One reason why supply now exceeds demand is that, contrary to expectation, the demand for labour in the part of the economy which is often, and confusingly, described as 'modern' has increased very little during the past ten to fifteen years. In some countries employment in enumerated enterprises, usually those which employ five or more persons, has hardly increased at all. In others, like those of East Africa, there have been years when employment has in fact decreased. Consequently, even without subscribing to the exaggerated assertions about urban unemployment, it may be legitimate to suppose that urban unemployment has been on the increase.

This is unexpected. In many of the low income countries, GDP has been increasing by 5–6 per cent a year and all past experience had seemed to indicate that increases in a country's GDP were associated with increases in employment. Unemployment did of course occur: mechanization created structural unemployment as when textile factories in England in the eighteenth century steadily eroded the livelihood of spinners and handloom weavers. It was this type of sequence which caused Marx to believe that capital accumulation could never proceed fast enough to create employment for all who were being displaced by the new machines. However, in England during the first half of the nineteenth century employment increased at roughly the same rate as GNP and thereafter until 1914 by about half that rate. Even that would have been insufficient to create full employment had not migration to America provided jobs for the remainder.

In the present underdeveloped countries, there is no such safety valve. Population and labour force are increasing by 2–3 per cent a year but although in many of them GDP has been rising at consistently respectable rates, wage employment has stagnated.

Although unemployment is not confined to towns, its manifestation is particularly acute in the towns. The growth of urban unemployment is particularly perplexing not just because governments fear it most, but because in so far as employment opportunities have increased, this has been principally in the towns, and this seems at first sight incompatible with growing urban unemployment.

The literature on economic development tends to gloss over

these problems with elegant disdain. Most of our development models, as we have seen, conceive economies as having two sectors: a subsistence sector, whose assumed and immutable attributes are sloth, tradition and backwardness, as well as being characterized by persistent 'disguised' unemployment; and a 'modern' sector of mines, plantations and especially industry. Development is then conceived to take the form of the enlargement of the modern sector through capital accumulation. The greater the will to develop, the greater will be the country's willingness to save and to transform its savings into capital. As capital accumulates so the modern sector grows, drawing in labour from the traditional sector until eventually there is none left and modernization is complete.

Such two-sector models appear to have little practical relevance, especially as it is common in low income countries for households to be in both sectors simultaneously – either because small farmers produce both for their own consumption and for the market, or because some members of a household are away from home, working for limited periods of time as wage earners in towns or in mines and plantations.

But if it were true in some very abstract sense that economic development followed such a two-sector path, then it makes the present very slow expansion of wage employment all the more serious, since it would seem to imply an indefinite postponement of the final goal when the whole economy is – as one might say – 'modern'.

Why have employment opportunities increased so slowly? It is often said to be a result of technological changes that have their origin in the advanced industrial countries, where the factor proportions between capital and labour are reversed and advances in technology make production processes ever more capital intensive. Developing countries are said to have no choice but to use these technologies. They could of course use obsolete machines but, so the argument runs, to do so is to court disaster in competition with countries that use the latest technologies. It may even turn out to be a false economy if later it proves difficult to obtain spare parts. Many go further and argue that in the West greater capital intensity has been the cause and effect of the high real income of wage earners. It is said to be a cause because high wages make employers look for ways of displacing expensive labour by cheaper machines, and it is a consequence because the machines enable labour to produce so much more. The argument then shifts to underdeveloped countries where it is said that this technology, reflecting the industrial countries' factor proportions, is the one they *should* use because, if it maximizes output per worker in the West, it must do so equally in underdeveloped countries. If, as a result, the growth of manufacturing creates little additional employment, this is treated as part of the order of nature and shrugged off as one of those unfortunate but inevitable concomitants of industrialization which, from all other points of view, surely bestows inestimable benefits!

This line of reasoning is very appealing to those who are reluctant to consider the possibility that what is here attributed to well-nigh immutable forces may, in fact, be susceptible to modification by the adoption of appropriate government *policies*. When one recalls that there are very few underdeveloped countries in which 'industrial' employment accounts for more than 10 per cent of total employment, it must appear improbable that these technological developments can explain more than a small part of the failure of total employment to rise. Even if it is true that prospective manufacturers have often little choice of machines available to them, this is not because more labour intensive machinery would now be uneconomical to users in developing countries, but simply because it would be uneconomical in countries where wages are high, and, as we saw in an earlier chapter, these are the countries for which the machine makers principally produce.

If the stagnation in employment cannot be ascribed primarily to technological factors but is rather the result of measures of policy, what are the policies in question which seem to positively *encourage* the adoption of capital intensive techniques?

First, there is the provision of *either* very generous investment allowances or even of capital grants. In Uganda, for instance, firms were able to write off 120 per cent of capital expenditure in the year in which it was incurred. Development Area Policy in this country has followed a similar pattern, but the last Government recognized the need to counterbalance the measures tending towards capital intensity by the introduction of the Regional Employment Premium. None of the low income countries have done likewise. The justification of giving fiscal encouragement to capital intensive forms of investment is, of course, that anything which will encourage capital investment will *ipso facto* promote employment. But as we have seen, both overseas and in the Development Areas in this country, given inappropriate technologies, the amount of employment created may be very small.

Another example is the failure to give adequate inducement for training of skilled labour. It is often said, rightly, that one major reason for choosing a mechanical rather than a manual process is a shortage of people with the necessary skills. This has been acknowledged for decades but if it continues to be a problem it may be that the explanation is that firms find it cheaper to buy machines than to train staff. Governments could counteract this by treating training as an 'allowable expense' in computing income tax, or better still, pay for the cost of training and finance it by a levy on industry as a whole.

Most important in stemming the tide to labour-saving techniques are policies which will check increases in wages. Employment may *not* be a function of the *absolute level* of wages, but few would deny the effect of the *rate of change* of wages. If that is rapid it will almost certainly cause employers to economize in the use of labour.

This can be illustrated with reference to the table on page 137 which relates changes in employment to changes in wages in a number of African countries; the negative correlation is very marked.

The reasons for these rapid increases in pay, especially in the newly independent countries of Africa, are an amalgam of greater trade union bargaining power and of what Lewis (1965) has described as a 'more powerful social conscience among capitalists', which makes them very ready to agree to wage increases especially in the many industries which enjoy some form of monopoly power, and where either a reduction in profits is regarded as a price worth paying for industrial and political peace or where increased wage costs can be

Table 1 **Annual percentage changes in African employment and real wages,** *circa* **1954–64**

	Employment	Wages
Tanzania	−2·6	14·1
Uganda	−0·6	8·2
Zambia	0·0	8·0
Kenya	0·7	3·4
Rhodesia	1·2	3·5
Ghana	6·9	3·0

Source: Robson and Lury (eds.) (1969, p. 62).

passed on to the consumer. Lastly, especially in the early post-independence years, governments quite deliberately either raised wages or instituted wage fixing machinery which would have that effect. It was widely felt that, to quote the slightly unfortunate words of the Uganda Minimum Wage Advisory Board Report of 1964, unskilled workers were 'underfed, underhoused and underclothed', and that it was 'of paramount importance to the country's future stability and prosperity that we achieve, as rapidly as possible, a wage structure based on the needs of the family unit' (Frank, 1968).

One can differ as to whether it is preferable to go for a policy which maximizes the growth of employment opportunities or to have a small but prosperous proletariat. What cannot be at issue is that these are to some extent mutually exclusive policy goals, that there is a trade-off between them and that, by and large, rising wages will tend to have the effect of encouraging economy in the use of labour. In the public sector this is because in most underdeveloped countries 60–80 per cent of government expenditure is on wages and salaries and consequently the number who can be employed is inversely related to their pay for any given level of tax revenue. In private *industry* it may make least difference in existing firms, but over the rest of the private sector a rapid rise in wages will tend to lead to the substitution of capital.

In some situations to produce a given output with less labour need be no catastrophe, as when either, for example, inefficiencies of management are eliminated, or to choose another example, people remain longer in employment and thus become more proficient. But in neither of these examples has labour been replaced by capital. What is more questionable is to replace domestic staff by washing machines or porters by forklift trucks. It may make perfectly good sense to the housewife or the employer, but there is likely to be something very wrong with economic policy if it *does*, especially in countries which are trying to hold imports down.

A third example of policy measures which lead to inappropriate capital intensity lies in the field of foreign aid: Donors of foreign aid hardly help the pursuit of sensible policies if they insist upon confining their aid to the foreign exchange components of projects. Who will pay unemployed people to build roads, if imported earth-moving equipment can be obtained free?

In sum, an answer to the question why the number of new jobs has risen so slowly cannot be couched convincingly in terms of technological inevitability alone, but must also refer to misguided economic policies.

This raises another question: can one in fact hope for a fall in urban unemployment, if by the pursuit of different policies one was successful in creating a greater number of additional jobs? On the face of it this question must seem paradoxical, since one, not unnaturally, takes it for granted that *more* jobs mean less unemployment. But the answer is not so straightforward, for unemployment will only fall if the numbers entering the towns do not increase.

The large gap between rural and urban pay in favour of the latter, is in itself quite enough to explain migration to towns in search of work. But this migration is not solely a function of pay differentials, but is also partly a function of the *probability* of finding a job (Todaro, 1969). People are quite realistic about the likelihood that they will not find a job at once; they realize that they will have to wait, and how many go depends in part on how long it may take to find one's first job. In other words, urban migration is in part a function of the probability of finding a job, or of finding it in a given time, and that in turn depends on the existing level of unemployment, the rate at which people leave their jobs, and the rate of job creation. Consequently it may well be that if the rate of job creation increases, this will *not* reduce urban unemployment because as soon as it becomes known that jobs have become easier to get, the flow of migrants to the towns increases, thus replenishing the 'pool' of urban unemployed – and this without any change in income differential between town and country.

Some evidence of this exists from Nairobi at the time of the 1964 Tripartite Agreement, under which private employers and the Government agreed to increase the numbers of employees on their payrolls by 15 per cent at once, on condition that trade unions agreed to accept a wage moratorium. In the event, the Government could not afford to increase its labour force, but private employers *did* and this was said to act like a magnet attracting new workers into the urban labour market (Todaro, 1969).

This analysis points to the recognition that urban unemployment cannot be tackled solely by changes in policy designed to increase the number of urban jobs. As we saw earlier, part of the problem arises from the fact that pay either is, or appears to be, much higher in the towns than in the countryside and thus draws ever greater numbers to the towns. The answer here lies not in policies to stimulate urban employment but rather in measures to make rural areas more attractive and thus to reduce the pull of towns. So long as the great majority live in the rural areas the task of improving the productivity of agriculture and of providing greater amenities must in any case be the main concern of governments. This is, of course, not incompatible with ensuring that wherever there is a choice of policies, the one which creates more jobs is preferred – whether it be in the towns or in the countryside.

The chapter began with a caution about the use of the term 'employment' in economies where the majority earn their living in ways other than as wage earners. In the last few years, much more attention has been given to this and it is becoming increasingly recognized that since wage earning is only one way of earning a living the proper way to think of 'employment' is to let that term encompass *all* activities by which people earn a living, whether it be on small farms, in trade, handicrafts or by any other means. The International Labour Office's World Employment Programme, and especially the study undertaken under its auspices in Kenya, has been influential in propagating this new way of viewing 'employment', and this has in turn led to new policy proposals.[1]

Throughout this book we have treated as axiomatic that the aim of economic development is to make the majority of people better off, or to raise their real incomes. One way of doing so would be by lowering the prices of the goods consumed by the majority. But the policy of developing industries by restricting competing imports has generally had an opposite effect. The other way to raise real incomes is to provide more opportunities to small-scale producers working in what the ILO Report on Kenya describes as the 'informal sector', which it contrasts with those employed in statistically enumerated concerns, the 'formal sector' comprising large businesses and government employment. The 'informal sector' contains village builders and craftsmen, small furniture workshops, makers of paraffin lamps from discarded tins or charcoal braziers from scrap metal; barbers operating in the open air; 'roadside Hiltons' providing tea and a hunk of bread under a tinned roof and on plain wooden benches; transporters, traders, hawkers and photographers.

One could list dozens of other, similar, activities. What all have in common is that they operate on a very small scale, that they use only hand tools and are therefore very labour intensive, and that they mostly cater for a low income market where price matters more than an elegant finish. Those work-

1. *Employment, incomes and equality: a strategy for increasing productive employment in Kenya*: International Labour Office, Geneva 1972.

ing in this informal sector tend to be at a disadvantage. Unlike the large factories, they receive no protection from competing imports or Government assistance of any kind and, being generally unable to borrow, have to provide working capital out of their own savings. Worse, especially in Africa, they are often deliberately discriminated against on the grounds that their methods of production are primitive and that they often work under primitive conditions. Governments are inclined to believe that things produced in 'modern' hygienic factories must do more to promote development. This is mistaken economic analysis. Things produced with simple implements and in premises that may consist of no more than a tin roof on wooden poles economize on fixed capital, if nothing else. Arguably they may absorb more inputs per unit of output, but some of these inputs, like discarded tins or tyres would have no alternative uses whilst the people working in the concerns manifestly lack alternative employment opportunities yielding higher incomes. There is also clearly a market for the things produced or these activities would not take place. To discriminate against such activities is to mistake the symptoms of poverty for their cause. The informal sector exists because countries are poor; it helps to reduce their poverty, by providing productive employment and a source of income to those who have no better alternative. It is not easy to see what Governments could do actively to promote this form of economic activity, but they could at least refrain from harassing those whose livelihoods depend upon it.

10 In Conclusion

The previous chapter stopped short of one question which it may be well to raise to conclude this book: is there perhaps a policy conflict between maximizing employment and maximizing GNP? In an earlier chapter we saw that most of the development models are in some way concerned with the question of how to raise the proportion of income which is reinvested and we found a substantial consensus that the greater the share of income which accrues to potential investors, the higher the probable rate of development. A capital intensive technology which minimizes distribution of income to employees will appear in this context to maximize growth. But this cannot be true in market economies in which a part of the incentive to invest must come from the anticipation of rising consumer expenditure. Since consumer expenditure will be positively correlated with employment there may be no real conflict between maximizing employment and maximizing income in the long-run because the increase in purchasing power generated by rising employment will in the long-run also maximize the national income by providing the necessary incentives to invest. Contrary to many of the more mechanical theories of economic development, future consumption is *not* necessarily enhanced by present abstinence and the exhortations to save and to channel resources into the hands of governments or entrepreneurs has often done no more than create an illusion of development without really raising standards of life. Widespread gains in current incomes will do more than forced saving to enhance meaningful development, because a rising standard of life *now* is a surer way to greater future prosperity than years of misery for the majority whilst a small elite of capitalists, civil servants or highly paid wage earners enjoy a standard of life that is unattainable for the rest. In the words of Francis Bacon –

'Money is like muck, not good except it be spread'!

References

Note: The page number(s) following each entry refer to the pages in this book on which the work is cited.

AGARWALA, A. N., and SINGH, S. P. (eds.) (1963), *Economics of Underdevelopment*, Galaxy Books. (65)

BAER, W. (1965), *Industrialization and Economic Development in Brazil*, Yale University Press. (98)

BALDWIN, R. E. (1966), *Economic Development and Export Growth: A Study of Northern Rhodesia 1920–60*, University of California Press. (35, 45)

BALOGH, T., and STREETEN, P. P. (1963), 'The co-efficient of ignorance', *Bull. of the Oxford University Institute of Statistics*, vol. 25, no. 2, pp. 97–107. (22)

BARANSON, V. J. (1967), *Manufacturing Problems in India: The Cummins Diesel Experience*, Syracuse University Press. (94)

BAUER, P. T. (1957), *Economic Analysis and Underdeveloped Countries*, Cambridge University Press. (12, 68)

BAUER, P. T. (1959), 'International economic development', *Economic J.*, vol. 69, no. 273, pp. 105–23. (12, 31, 32)

BAUER, P. T. (1965), 'The vicious circle of poverty', *Weltwirtschaftliches Archiv.*, vol. 95, no. 2; reprinted in I. Livingstone (ed.), *Economic Policy for Development*, Penguin, 1971. (12, 28)

BAUER, P. T., and YAMEY, B. S. (1957), *Economics of Underdeveloped Countries*, Cambridge University Handbooks. (64)

BECKERMAN, W. (1966), *International Comparisons of Real Income*, OECD. (19)

BOEKE, J. H. (1953), *Economics and Economic Policy of Dual Societies*, Institute of Pacific Relations. (34, 35)

BOSE, S., and CLARK, E. H. (1969), 'Some basic considerations on agricultural mechanization in West Pakistan', *Pakistan Development Review*, pp. 272–308. (114)

BROWN, L. R. (1970), *Seeds of Change: The Green Revolution and Development in the 1970s*, Praeger. (111, 114, 116)

BRUTON, H. (1968), 'Import substitution and productivity growth', *Journal of Development Studies*, vol. 14, no. 3, pp. 306–26. (99)

CAINE, Sir S. (1966), *Prices for Primary Producers*, Hobart Paper no. 24, Institute of Economic Affairs, 2nd edn. (52)

CAIRNCROSS, Sir A. K. (1962), *Factors in Economic Development*, Allen & Unwin. (51)

CHAUDHURI, P. (1971), *Aspects of Indian Economic Development: A Book of Readings*, Allen & Unwin. (107)

ELKAN, W. (1958), 'The East African trade in woodcarvings', *Africa*, vol. 28, no. 4, pp. 314–23, reprinted in R. W. Clower and Harry Townsend, *The Art of Economics*, Penguin, 1974. (38)

ELKAN, W. (1960), *Migrants and Proletarians: Urban Labour in the Economic Development of Uganda*, OUP. (38)

ELLIS, H. S., and WALLICH, H. C. (eds.) (1961), *Economic Development for Latin America*, St Martin's Press. (24)

ENKE, S., and ZIND, R. G. (1969), 'Effect of fewer births on average income', *J. of Biosocial Science*, vol. 1, no. 1, (125, 126)

FEI, J. C. H., and RANIS, G. (1964), *Development of the Labour Surplus Economy: Theory and Policy*, Irwin. (68)

FRANK, C. A. Jr (1968), 'Urban unemployment and economic growth in Africa', *Oxford Economic Papers*, vol. 2, no. 2, pp. 250–74. (137)

GALBRAITH, J. K. (1965), *The Underdeveloped Country*, Canadian Broadcasting Corporation. (39)

GALENSON, W., and LEIBENSTEIN, H. (1955), 'Investment criteria, productivity and economic development', *Q. J. of Economics*, vol. 69, no. 3, pp. 343–71. (86, 87)

GATT (1959), *International Trade*, GATT. (92)

GERSCHENKRON, A. (1965), *Economic Backwardness in Historical Perspective*, Praeger. (85)

GERSCHENKRON, A. (1968), *Continuity in History and other Essays*, Harvard University Press. (34)

HAGEN, E. E. (1964), *On the Theory of Social Change: How Economic Growth Begins*, Tavistock Publications. (33, 34)

HAZELWOOD, A. (ed.) (1967), *African Integration and Disintegration: Case Studies in Economic and Political Union*, OUP. (100)

HICKS, J. R. (1939), *Value and Capital*, OUP. (122)

HIGGINS, B. (1956), 'The dualistic theory of underdeveloped areas', *Economic Development and Cultural Change*, January, pp. 99–112.(36)

HILL, P. (1963), *Migrant Cocoa Farmers in Southern Ghana*, Cambridge University Press. (68)

HIRSCHMAN, A. O. (1958), *Strategy of Economic Development*, Yale University Press. (23, 69, 82, 83, 121, 122)

HIRSCHMAN, A. O. (ed.) (1961), *Latin American Issues*, Twentieth Century Fund. (24)

HOOLEY, R. W. (1967), 'Measurement of capital formation in underdeveloped countries', *Review of Economics and Statistics*, vol. 49, pp. 199–208. (21)

HOSELITZ, B. F. (1957), 'Non-economic factors in economic development', *American Economic Review*, vol. 47, pp. 28–41. (33)

Hsu, F. L. K. (1954), 'Cultural factors', in H. F. Williamson and
J. A. Buttrick (eds.), *Economic Development: Principles and
Patterns*, Prentice-Hall. (20)

IBRD (1970), *World Bank Atlas: Population, Per Capita Product
and Growth Rates*, Washington DC. (17)

Jacobson, H. L. (1969), 'Export opportunities for developing
countries', *Progress*, no. 4. (101)

Johnson, H. G. (1966), 'Trade preferences and developing
countries', *Lloyds Bank Review*, no. 80, pp. 1–18. (97)

Jorgensen, D. (1967), 'Testing alternative theories of the
development of a dual economy', in I. Adelman and E. Thorbecke
(eds.), *The Theory and Design of Economic Development*,
Johns Hopkins. (70)

Kaplinsky, R. (1970), *Aspects of the Relationship between Import
Substitution and Industrialization in Underdeveloped Countries*,
University of Sussex. (92)

Kilby, P. (1969), *Industrialization in an Open Economy:
Nigeria 1945–66*, OUP. (94)

Killick, T. (1967), 'Commodity agreements and international aid',
Westminster Bank Review, February, pp. 18–30. (55)

Kindleberger, C. P. (1965), *Economic Development*, McGraw Hill,
2nd edn. (24)

Kravis, I. B. (1970), 'Trade as a handmaiden of growth:
similarities between the nineteenth and twentieth centuries',
Econ. J. vol. 80, no. 320, pp. 850–72. (50)

Lary, H. B. (1968), *Imports of Manufactures from Less
Developed Countries*, National Bureau of Economic Research. (102)

Leibenstein, H. (1963), *Economic Backwardness and
Economic Growth*, Wiley Science Editions. (81)

Leibenstein, H. (1969), 'Pitfalls in benefit-cost analysis of birth
prevention', *Population Studies*, vol. 23, no. 2, pp. 161–170. (127)

Lewis, S. R. (1969), *Economic Policy and Industrial Growth
in Pakistan*, Allen & Unwin. (97)

Lewis, Sir W. A. (1953), *Industrialization and Gold Coast*,
Government Printer, Accra. (65)

Lewis, Sir W. A. (1954), 'Economic development with unlimited
supplies of labour', *Manchester School*, May; reprinted in
A. N. Agarwala and S. P. Singh (eds.), *Economics of
Underdevelopment*, Galaxy Books, 1963. (63, 65)

Lewis, Sir W. A. (1955), *Theory of Economic Growth*,
Allen & Unwin. (80)

Lewis, Sir W. A. (1965), 'Unemployment in the developing areas',
in *Proceedings of the Third Biennial Midwest Research Conference
on Underdeveloped Areas*, Aldine Press. (136)

Lipsey, R. G. (1966), *Introduction to Positive Economics*,
Weidenfeld & Nicolson. (40, 61)

LIPTON, M. (1968), 'The theory of the optimizing peasant',
J. of Development Studies, vol. 4, no. 3, pp. 327–51. (39)

LITTLE, I., SCITOVSKY, T., and SCOTT, M. (1970), *Industry and
Trade in Some Developing Countries: A Comparative Study*,
OUP for OECD. (100)

LIVINGSTONE, I. (ed.) (1971), *Economic Policy for Development*,
Penguin. (57, 70)

LOWRY, J. H. (1970), *World Population and Food Supply*,
Edward Arnold. (106)

MACBEAN, A. I. (1966), *Export Instability and Economic
Development*, Allen & Unwin. (53, 57, 58)

McCLELLAND, D. C. (1961), *The Achieving Society*,
Van Nostrand. (33)

MEIER, G. M. (1963), *International Trade and Development*, Harper
& Row. (12)

MEIER, G. M. (1970), *Leading Issues in Economic Development*,
OUP, 2nd edn. (12, 18, 19, 44)

MITCHELL, F. (1970), 'The value of tourism in East Africa',
Eastern Africa Econ. Rev., vol. 2, no. 1, pp. 1–21. (27)

MYINT, H. (1954), 'An interpretation of economic backwardness',
Oxford Economic Papers, June; reprinted in Myint,
Economic Theory and the Underdeveloped Countries, OUP, 1971. (32)

MYINT, H. (1967), *The Economics of Developing Countries*,
Hutchinson University Library, 3rd edn. (41, 71)

MYRDAL, G. (1963), *Economic Theory and Underdeveloped Regions*,
Methuen University Paperbacks. (24, 25, 29, 31, 42, 43, 116)

NATH, S. K. (1962), 'The theory of balanced growth',
Oxford Economic Papers, vol. 14, no. 2, pp. 138–53. (80)

NEUMARK, S. D. (1958), 'Economic development and economic
incentives', *South African J. of Economics*, vol. 26, no. 1,
pp. 55–63. (38)

NEWMAN, P. (1965), *Malaria Eradication and Population Growth –
with special reference to Ceylon and British Guiana*, University of
Michigan Press. (120)

NULTY, L. E. (1972), *The Green Revolution in West Pakistan*,
Praeger. (112, 115)

NURKSE, R. (1953), *Problems of Capital Formation in
Underdeveloped Countries*, OUP. (28, 71, 80)

OHLIN, G. (1967), *Population Control and Economic Development*,
OECD Development Centre. (119, 120, 124, 125)

PACK, H., and TODARO, M. P. (1969), 'Technological transfer,
labour absorption and economic development',
Oxford Economic Papers, vol. 21, no. 3, pp. 395–403. (90)

PEARSON, L. B. (chairman) (1969), *Partners in Development:
Report of the Commission on International Development*
('Pearson Report'), Pall Mall. (16, 22, 110, 116)

PINCUS, J. (1967), *Trade, Aid and Development*, McGraw Hill. (84)

PREBISCH, R. (1950), *The Economic Development of Latin America and its Principal Problems*, UN. (45, 46, 47)

RANIS, G., and FEI, J. C. H. (1961), 'A theory of economic development', *Amer. Econ. Rev.*, vol. 51, no. 4, pp. 533–58. (68)

RANIS, G., and FEI, J. C. H. (1964), *Development of the Labour Surplus Economy: Theory and Policy*, Irwin. (68)

ROBSON, P. (1968), *Economic Integration in Africa*, Allen & Unwin. (100)

ROBSON, P. (ed.) (1972), *Economics of International Integration*, Penguin. (100)

ROBSON, P., and LURY, D. (eds.) (1969), *The Economics of Africa*, Allen & Unwin. (137)

ROSENSTEIN-RODAN, P. (1943), 'Problems of industrialization of Eastern and South-Eastern Europe', *Econ. J.*, June; reprinted in A. N. Agarwala and S. P. Singh (eds.), *Economics of Underdevelopment*, Galaxy Books, 1963. (71, 78)

ROSENSTEIN-RODAN, P. (1961), 'Notes on the theory of the big push' in H. S. Ellis and H. C. Wallich (eds.), *Economic Development for Latin America*, St Martin's Press. (78, 79)

ROSTOW, W. W. (1960), *Stages of Economic Growth*, Cambridge University Press. (81)

SAMUELSON, P. A. (1948), 'International trade and the equalization of factor prices', *Econ. J.*, June, pp. 163–84. (48)

SCHATZ, S. P. (1965), 'Achievement and economic growth: a critique', *Q. J. of Econ.*, vol. 79, no. 2, pp. 234–41. (33)

SCHULTZ, T. W. (1956), 'Role of government in promoting economic growth', in L. D. White (ed.), *The State of the Social Sciences*, Chicago University Press. (70)

SEN, A. K. (1968), *Choice of Techniques*, Blackwell, 3rd edn. (72)

SINGER, H. W. (1964), *International Development: Growth and Change*, McGraw Hill. (81)

SINGER, H. W. (1970), 'Brief note on unemployment rates in developing countries', *Manpower and Unemployment Research in Africa*, vol. 3, no. 1. (130)

TODARO, M. P. (1969), 'A model of labour migration and urban unemployment in less developed countries', *Amer. Econ. Rev.*, vol. 59, no. 1, pp. 138–48. (138, 139)

TODARO, M. P. (1970), 'Some thoughts on the transfer of technology', *Eastern Africa Economic Review*, vol. 2, no. 1, pp. 53–64. (90)

TURNHAM, D. (1971), *The Employment Problem in Less Developed Countries: A Review of Evidence*, OECD Development Centre. (130)

UN (1971), *Monthly Bulletin of Statistics*, December. (24)

UNITED NATIONS ECONOMIC COMMISSION FOR LATIN AMERICA (1950), *Economic Survey of Latin America, 1949*, UN New York. (45)

150 References

UNITED NATIONS INDUSTRIAL DEVELOPMENT
ORGANIZATION (1969), *Industrial Development Survey*, vol. 1,
UN New York. (22)

WHARTON, C. R. Jr (1969), 'The green revolution: cornucopia
or pandora's box?', *Foreign Affairs*, vol. 47, pp. 68–9. (112, 113)

WILSON, T., SINHA, R. P., and CASTREE, J. R. (1969),
'The income terms of trade of developed and developing
countries', *Economic Journal*, vol. 79, pp. 813–32. (49)

Index

Note: References to authors have been omitted from this Index and appear instead at the end of the relevant entry in the list of References.

More about Penguins
and Pelicans

Penguinews, which appears every month, contains details of all the new books issued by Penguins as they are published. From time to time it is supplemented by *Penguins in Print*, which is our complete list of almost 5,000 titles.

A specimen copy of *Penguinews* will be sent to you free on request. Please write to Dept EP, Penguin Books Ltd, Harmondsworth, Middlesex, for your copy.

In the U.S.A.: For a complete list of books available from Penguins in the United States write to Dept CS, Penguin Books, 625 Madison Avenue, New York, New York 10022.

In Canada: For a complete list of books available from Penguins in Canada write to Penguin Books Canada Ltd, 2801 John Street, Markham, Ontario L3R 1B4.